Dedication

This book is dedicated to my Uncle Joey, who demonstrated love to all, and recognized **everyone** *as a child of God. It is a culmination of the many wonderful conversations we shared together, during both the best and the worst times of my life. After recognizing the effects of his healing words, I started to record them, so they would be indelibly imprinted in my memory. Joey has been a lifelong inspiration to me, and without him, this book would have never been written.*

Table of Contents

Acknowledgements v

Introduction ix

1. *What is OCD?* *1*
2. *Causes and Consequences of OCD* *15*
3. *My Personal Spiritual Journey* *23*
4. *Believe in God's Healing Power Within You* *37*
5. *Dealing with Legalism and Perfectionism* *47*
6. *Dealing with the Guilt Accompanying OCD* *61*
7. *Exaggerated Responsibility* *73*
8. *The Same Mind that Can Make You Sick Can Make You Well* *81*
9. *Challenge and Analyze Your OCD* *107*
10. *You Are Destined for Peace* *141*
11. *Medication and My Experience with It* *161*
12. *Cognitive Behavioral Therapy* *181*
13. *Afterword – My Life Today* *199*
14. *Sayings Worth Remembering* *207*

Works Cited 211

Acknowledgements

I would like to thank God, who has provided me with all the love, forgiveness and courage to heal from OCD. He has been, and always will be my ultimate healer and support.

I would also especially like to thank my Uncle Joey. Without him, I would not be alive and well today. He saw to it that I cultivated the tools within myself needed to combat this unrelenting, horrible illness. His insight and suggestions on how to deal with OCD have been nothing short of brilliant. From him, I learned to analyze the thoughts that come into my mind, and to treasure what I have long sought after: the peace that passes all human understanding. Without a doubt, he is the wisest and most loving person that I have ever met. Before the completion of this book, Joey passed away in 2016 at the age of 96. Yet, his inspirational voice and spirit continue to live on.

I also thank my husband, who has put up with me through more than thirty years of marriage and has come a long way in his understanding of mental illness. He knew I was suffering from OCD long before I ever did. He also made many attempts in trying to logically talk me out of some of the irrational OCD fears over the years. At the beginning, I dismissed his suggestions. Later on, I began to see just how insightful he really was. My husband's love was unwavering as he supported me financially and emotionally; he also edited this manuscript.

I am blessed by our two daughters, who make me very proud because of the exceptional individuals they truly are. I love them; they have given my life purpose and meaning. One of my daughters, Annie (now an attorney), also spent countless hours reading and editing this book. Many of her perceptive suggestions were implemented, which led to an improved manuscript incorporating some of her recollections. My younger daughter Tammie, an engineer, is a trustworthy thought partner and problem solver, much like her father, and someone whom I can always trust and depend on.

I owe a big thank you to Joey's niece, Fran. She gave me emotional support and comfort during the darkest hours of my life. Fran prepared meal after meal and encouraged me to eat when I lost my appetite due to obsessive worry. Her cheery, positive attitude, even during adverse circumstances, and her love of life has become a model for me to emulate. Fran also helped edit this book and I cannot repay her for the help and time she has spent on this project.

Another person who helped me enormously is Nan DeBlase, a humorous, creative writer and poet. I feel privileged not only to have Nan as a friend, but as my

Acknowledgements

primary editor and supporter, who critically read this manuscript several times, challenged me on its contents, and played a pivotal role in the revision process.

My dear, childhood friend of over forty years, Vicky, visited me every single day during the time I was hospitalized. After I was released, I was still sorely underweight and had little appetite. Both Vicky and her partner encouraged me to leave the house, treated me to many delicious lunches, and motivated me to participate in life again. I will be eternally grateful for their friendship.

I find the saying, "If you want something done, ask a busy person to do it" to be true. I must express my heartfelt gratitude to my friend Judy K., who is one of the hardest workers I know; she took me to my first 12 step support group, and researched OCD for me when I was not up to the task myself. Suffice it to say that I did not even have to ask for Judy's help; she knew exactly what to do in a crisis situation.

Last but not least, I would like to thank my previous next-door neighbor, Judy F., who was a role model to me in how to be an exemplary human being. She embodied the essence of goodness and impressed me with her attitude that the giving of our service to others is a reward (and a privilege) in and of itself.

I suffered through many sleepless nights, terrorizing thoughts and fears, depression, loss of appetite, and would not wish this kind of anguish on anyone. Having said this, however, I will admit that undergoing the process of combating obsessive compulsive disorder led me into a wonderful relationship with God and has made me a better and more spiritual person. I am finally free of an enslaving thought process and am experiencing true peace despite challenging circumstances at times. I look forward to my continuing spiritual journey and becoming the best possible person, I can be.

Introduction

I have lived in two worlds; the one of normalcy, and the one of mental illness. As a child I remember being higher strung and more risk adverse than my peers, and in some ways socially awkward. I was the only child of immigrant and uneducated parents, and at the age of ten, in 1967, my father died. He had a two-year bout with lung cancer, which wiped out my mother financially and emotionally.

In August of 1967, I became a latch key kid, with a literal key around my neck, and little parental supervision. My mother, who had no opportunity for an education beyond the seventh grade, was compelled to work as a seamstress for minimum wage in order to pay the bills and put food on our table. Despite unfavorable conditions, she tried her very best to raise and support her only child. She had only one expectation of me – that I do well in school and become educated, so that my life would not be filled with stress and struggle, as hers was. Although my mother fought to balance her job at work and raise a child alone, she never asked me to cook meals or do household chores. I became an honor student in high school, and then graduated from a local college magna cum laude with a degree in biology. My mother remained a widow, never remarrying, devoting her life to my upbringing.

I became a teacher and taught biology and chemistry for nine years while also marrying, and subsequently becoming pregnant with my first child, showing relatively few signs of OCD before this time. It was a very difficult pregnancy from the second to the fifth month, at which time I started to experience irrational fears, panic attacks, inability to sleep, and general depression. My husband was a full-time student obtaining his Master's degree in mathematics, while I was miserable, pregnant, and working to support the both of us. After the fifth month of pregnancy, I recovered psychologically and eventually gave birth to our first daughter. I was able to stay home full time, since by then, my husband had graduated and found employment as an actuary in the insurance industry. My daughter was born with a cleft lip and palate and required a great deal of care. When she was an infant, my repetitive checking of doors, windows, and appliances began, especially at night. I gave birth to my second daughter about three years later. My fears multiplied, and my days became anxiety ridden. Of course, parents are normally concerned about the safety of their children and a certain amount of concern is reasonable. But in my case, my worries became paralyzing, exaggerated, and led to sleeping difficulties. In fact, many of my routines escalated at bedtime, for the purpose of "calming myself down" so that I could finally get to sleep. Panic attacks

Introduction

returned. What was an ordinary amount of stress for some people became devastating for me.

During all of my ongoing problems I did not realize how lucky I was to be able to confide in an understanding uncle, Joey, who began to introduce me to spirituality. With his help, I recovered from the panic attacks, and led a relatively normal life. I was able to return to work on a per diem basis as an educational consultant when my children were both in elementary school. At the age of forty-nine, one year before my youngest daughter graduated high school, I successfully returned to teaching full time. By the following year, however, I entered into menopause, and my OCD routines increased dramatically. I experienced panic attacks and depression to the point that I needed to be hospitalized after I confessed to my trusted uncle that I was suicidal, and actually asked him to help me end my life. I was seriously ill, and was forced to acknowledge, without a shadow of a doubt, that I had obsessive-compulsive disorder. I sought medical help and took psychotropic medication for the first time. Nevertheless, I was very opposed to medication or drugs of any kind.

After my hospital stay, I was sent to a therapist who was not very knowledgeable in treating OCD. At this point, my OCD symptoms were disabling: I could not drive or take care of my family. I had pre-sleep anxiety, my teaching career was terminated, and I had a great deal of trouble executing the usual requisites for daily life.

However, I again was able to confide in my understanding Uncle Joey and felt comfortable revealing my fears and rituals without any fear of judgment. He re-introduced me to spirituality, only this time, it was highly upgraded, and I became very receptive, probably because of the severity of my problem. God blessed me by placing him in my life, since the consequences of my OCD at this point were preventing me from functioning normally.

By reading and learning about OCD and practicing spirituality simultaneously, I began to recover. I was tremendously relieved to find out that OCD was actually a neurobiological brain disorder, rather than a personal weakness. I also eventually found a compassionate psychiatrist and a therapist more knowledgeable in OCD issues. I began pursuing God with my heart, mind and soul. Spirituality addressed some of my very worst fears, and the guilt and self-condemnation that usually accompanies OCD. My thyroid stimulating hormone and anxiety levels miraculously decreased. I was fighting a battle every day, however, I made steady progress.

What I learned from this experience was that while I had the propensity to worry obsessively, I also had the ability to be serene. I found out that my thoughts were making me sick, not events. At the peak of my OCD illness, thoughts fused into events in my mind. I had a

Introduction

tendency to be irrational, but I also had the capacity to apply logic. After some struggle, I finally realized that my fears and guilt were false, my concerns highly exaggerated and in most cases, trivial to anyone with a sound perspective. I learned that I had a healing power within me which I could draw upon when necessary, thus aiding my recovery.

I had to learn new ways of thinking, and as a result, grew spiritually in the process. Spiritual principles which I had heard before and ignored, suddenly became highly profound. With the help of God, my family members and the medical establishment, I was finally able to achieve what I sought – peace and serenity. This required, and still requires a tremendous commitment on my part. However, it is worth every minute of effort I spend pursuing this endeavor. Looking back, I wasted an excessive amount of time suffering needlessly. My only regret in life is not absorbing and applying spiritual principles sooner.

The good news is that if I could recover, so can you. You have the same healing power inside of yourself. It is my greatest wish to share what I have learned, so that you too, dear reader, can experience a rebirth.

1

What is OCD?

At around the same time I went through menopause, I was hospitalized for anxiety, depression and suicidal tendencies, and was forced to admit that I had a serious problem. I had done some prior reading and gained enough insight at the time to know that I was suffering from something called obsessive compulsive disorder, or simply put, OCD. I was quite ashamed of this fact and made an overwhelming effort to keep it a secret. It becomes quite difficult to maintain a status of secrecy, however, when you leave your job, become suicidal, end up in a psychiatric ward, and cannot take care of your own family. Once out of the hospital I was fortunate to have had the time and support to recover. I made it my mission to find out what I could do about this illness and discovered quite a bit of encouraging literature. Thirty years ago, the medical prognosis for OCD was grim, since this disease was not well understood, and no good treatment was available (Osborn, 8). Times have changed and recent developments have dramatically altered the entire outlook for many sufferers, enabling them to recover and function normally.

The word "disease" correctly describes the nature

of OCD. It is certainly a "dis-ease," or uneasiness with oneself. Unfortunately, there is no simple test for OCD. One realizes whether he or she has the condition by the manifestation of "symptoms," which are obsessions and compulsions. Dr. Ian Osborne, a psychiatrist who himself had OCD, described the term obsession for the general public to mean preoccupation with something, or someone, such as a girl being obsessed with her looks, or a boy being obsessed with playing video games. A clinical obsession is something quite different. It is a battle for mind control, in which intrusive, unwanted and inappropriate thoughts cause marked anxiety and distress (Osborn, 30). Compulsions and rituals are what a person **does** to reduce the anxiety and stress caused by the obsessions (Osborn, 37).

  Compulsions can manifest themselves in a myriad of ways. For example, a fear of a burglary can lead to the repetitive checking of door locks and windows. Fears about potential fires in the home can lead to the excessive checking of stoves, ovens and electrical appliances. A morbid fear of germs and contamination can lead to endless washing and showering as well as other avoidance behaviors, such as refusing to shake another person's hand or using a public restroom. A desire to tap a particular number of times or count to a certain number in order to prevent some disaster (such as harm coming to a relative) would also be categorized as a compulsive ritual.

Dr. Steven Phillipson published an article in the OCD Newsletter, "Thinking the Unthinkable: Guilt beyond a Reasonable Doubt," stating that there are actually three types of OCD. The most familiar type is the OCD where rituals, such as checking door and window locks, faucets, and gas stoves are observable and are used by the sufferer to relieve anxiety. The second type of OCD, known as the pure obsessional, or pure O, is less common, and consists of unwanted, intrusive, repetitive, fearful, irrational thoughts without rituals. For example, a person may have a morbid fear of stabbing himself or others or jumping off a high place. The third type is called "responsibility OCD," whereby the individual feels an extraordinary and burdensome responsibility to prevent any harm, no matter how slight, to others or to himself. Dr. Jonathan Grayson refers to this as an "inflated sense of responsibility" in his book, *Freedom from Obsessive Compulsive Disorder* (100). No matter what the names or labels are, I personally have suffered from all three types.

Grayson points out that what lies behind OCD compulsions and rituals is a desire for absolute certainty, which is impossible (97). Looking back, I realize that I wanted absolute assurance that some imagined disaster would not happen, or that something was "totally safe." My frequent requests for reassurance from family members and my desire to control many aspects of a situation reflected this. Grayson points out that once we are able to "tolerate uncertainty," we can be well on our way toward recovery (58-59). Once I accepted uncertainty and understood that most of what I was worried about was outside my control anyway, I adopted an attitude of "whatever happens, happens," and over time, my condition improved dramatically.

I have included a list of behaviors and symptoms that summarize the scope of obsessive compulsive disorder, such as checking, contamination, and ordering compulsions, requests for reassurance, hoarding, and mental obsessions (Osborn, 39-42) and have outlined some of my own experiences.

Checking Compulsions

Checking compulsions is a hallmark OCD symptom. An individual will "check" a situation over and over in order to make sure that no harm will come to either himself or to another person. In my case, I became a "checker," and had compulsions to check door locks, windows, gas stoves, and the barbeque grill, just to name a few items on a very long list. In each case, the amount of time I devoted to such tasks was, in hindsight, highly unreasonable. It might be quite normal to check a door or window once after it was opened. However, I was checking

What is OCD?

windows multiple times that **I had never opened**! I might have opened one window during the day, yet I would feel compelled to check all of them, since I "might have" mistakenly checked the wrong window. The element of doubt fueled my compulsive behaviors, which were especially prevalent before bedtime.

    I felt compelled to check my garbage cans to see that they were tightly covered so that no protruding objects could "hurt" anyone and that no plastic bags could be carried by the wind to fly away and possibly suffocate some lone child. Electrical appliances, such as the toaster and the coffee maker, had to be checked to make sure that they were off and did not cause a fire and burn down the house. I did this even though I don't eat toast, nor do I drink coffee. This certainly sounds irrational, but I did not know it at the time. In my mind, perhaps someone else had used these appliances and left them plugged in, which could have resulted in a potential fire. The supposed catastrophic consequences would be my fault. It did not occur to me that most people do not unplug appliances immediately after using them. Nor did I think about the fact that I did not repeatedly check things for most of my life, and yet a "fire" never occurred in any of my residences. I was in full OCD mode and would do whatever was necessary to curtail the anxiety.

    I also felt compelled to make sure that I did not

leave the faucets running. A visual inspection was required, and I would stare at the faucet for several minutes. Then I put my hand underneath the faucet to make sure that I could not feel any water running just in case my visual inspection was wrong. When I attended public restrooms, I would still check the faucets in spite of the fact that some of the faucets did not have handles; they were of the "push type" where the water would run only when the faucet knobs were depressed. Yet I checked, thinking it was necessary, just in case the faucet knob failed mechanically. The same was true for public water fountains.

Over time, my list of repetitive checking grew exponentially. I developed an intense fear that I would inadvertently poison my precious dog. I checked the house to see that no vitamin or medicinal pills were left out, since they could theoretically harm her. I would check to see that the medicine bottles were securely fastened, and in a high cabinet, with its door securely shut. In hindsight, my dog did not like to swallow pills of any kind, since she made various attempts to spit them out the few times I had to give her prescribed medication from a veterinarian. (But she was known to snatch a chicken cutlet from the kitchen counter every so often when we were not watching.) Again, I did not think of the rational evidence to counter my OCD thoughts – which overwhelmed me. Looking back, many of my thoughts were irrational, and I was oblivious to my own erroneous thinking.

There are many more "checking" compulsions that OCD sufferers can manifest. The following is a brief list of some that I have experienced:

- Inspecting and removing articles of clothing, bags, and towels away from radiators, because of "flammability issues."
- Repetitive checking to determine if residual glass fragments were left after an accidental glass breakage, long after I had cleaned them up.
- Checking flammable liquids in the basement, to make sure they were safely secured.
- Inspecting my home heating system to make sure it was free of obstructions, and that the water level in my burner gauge was at the appropriate height.
- Checking cigarettes on sidewalks, or candles in the home to make sure they were out.
- Circling around the block many times while driving in order to make sure that I had not hit anyone or anything.

Although the checking was an attempt (in my mind) to reduce the feasibility of a feared consequence, I repeated it so often that it became a waste of time. With the help of a therapist about two years after my diagnosis, I realized that my anxiety was the "trigger" and the checking was my "drug" in order to eliminate it. And just as you need more and more of a drug to achieve the same effect, I needed to check more and more often in order to alleviate my distress. If an OCD sufferer refrains from checking, her anxiety level rises temporarily. This feeling is quite terrifying, as I know all too well.

Contamination Compulsions

The washing of hands or excessive showering is a prevalent feature of OCD. Dr. Judith Rapoport, psychiatrist, OCD expert, and author of the book, *The Boy Who Could Not Stop Washing*, reports that an intense fear of contamination, germ exposure, or untidiness, seems to be a hallmark symptom of OCD. She estimates that about 80 percent of OCD sufferers attending her clinic experience washing or grooming rituals (85). It is normal to wash hands before eating, or after using a restroom. However, a person who has OCD and contamination fears may wash and scrub his hands until they are red and raw. He doubts that he washed thoroughly enough and may have "missed a spot." He may also avoid touching doorknobs, shaking hands, or using public restrooms because he is worried about being exposed to germs and getting sick. A girl may worry about getting AIDS from playing hand games in the schoolyard. A teenager may refuse to go bowling because she saw a white powder near the bowling ball that "may have been anthrax."

The late Howard Hughes, a moviemaker, aviator, entrepreneur and billionaire, developed such a severe germ and contamination phobia that he isolated himself, thus leading a lonely and reclusive life in his later years. Because he could afford to pay his staff a great deal of money to follow his exact instructions about opening cans, windows, doors, the handling of objects, and so on, he avoided confronting his irrational fears, and slipped into a life of narcotic drug addiction and misery (Osborn, 37-39). His wealth actually became a deterrent to any possible OCD recovery.

Interestingly enough, I did not have washing rituals, but suffered from several contamination fears – an example was the possibility of poisoning people during meal preparation. I feared that I "may" have left meat and/or eggs out too long, leaving harmful bacteria to multiply, making the end product toxic. Germs "could have been contracted" from my sink or hands to the food, and thereby "dangerous." In hindsight, there were many times that I threw away perfectly good food items because of the fear of harming others (as well as myself).

Ordering Compulsions

Here, the person develops a preoccupation with

arranging items until they are just perfect, or symmetrical. Many times, it is done until it feels "just right." Sometimes, a person may feel that "something bad" might happen if things are not just so, or very uncomfortable if things are not in their proper place. As a child, I would not step on a sidewalk crack in order to prevent a potential catastrophe. As an adult, I would check the four burners of my stove top in a very particular order.

Behavioral Compulsions – Requests for Reassurance

A type of behavioral compulsion is the constant asking of reassurance (Osborn, 41). This can be in the form of asking a family member, "Is everything OK?" or "Is the gas turned off?" I remember my bedtime ritual of checking the door, stove, patio door, refrigerator, and so on. After completing the ritual, I would still ask my husband, "Is the door locked?" He would say, "Yes." Yet after a minute or so, I would ask him the same question, at which point he would become somewhat annoyed. I would then ask, "Are you sure the door is locked?" In my mind, I had the never-ending doubt about whether or not I heard his response correctly. By the third time, he was quite angry. I just needed reassurance. Again. Anything to make that anxiety vanish. In the beginning, my husband would react by either becoming upset, or by performing the task for me, and saying, "I checked it already." It took quite a while for my husband to understand the nature of an OCD illness. This is probably fairly common among family members of OCD sufferers. Unfortunately, when a family member either becomes irritated or enables the sufferer, it generally makes matters worse. Over time, my husband learned to question me and discuss my fears more rationally, and he became an ultimate source of support.

Mental Obsessions

A sufferer imagines that harm could be done either to herself or someone else. The following are some of my personal examples:

- Fear of running someone over when I hit a bump in the road while driving. I would circle around several times, returning to the same spot, to reassure myself that I did not hit anyone.
- Feeling guilty upon encountering an animal lying in the middle of the road – I believed I either ran over it while driving, or it was suffering and I did nothing to help/rescue it. I did not even know if the animal was actually suffering, since I was not able to get out of the car at times and check.
- Gift giving, especially to younger children, was a very agonizing event. I would examine a toy

wrapped in a plastic covering and envision the child suffocating after wrapping her head with the plastic that accompanied the toy. The imaginary "disaster" would be my fault. Any toy with buttons or protruding small objects was immediately nixed as a gift, because they could theoretically be removed (or fall off) and be swallowed by the child. The fictional "death" would also be my fault.

Many of my mental obsessions focused around my two daughters, especially during the teen and young adult years. I was extremely anxious when they went out, and came home late, imagining that all sorts of "terrible" things were occurring. (They could be drinking, having sex, etc.) I would make frequent calls, try to set curfews (that were not adhered to), and become highly upset when they were not home at a particular time. Of course, this led to quite a bit of friction, since my older daughter was very intent on asserting her independence. Many times, I was not able to sleep unless I knew that they were home, safely in their rooms. My desire to control their behavior, just so that I could sleep and relax, was basically ineffective.

Hoarding

Hoarding is driven by an intense anxiety that the

sufferer might accidentally discard something important. There is a tendency to save items to the "nth" degree. A hoarder is afraid to throw anything away, so that junk mail or other items of no use to the owner would be saved anyway.

I remember helping a friend clear out her mother's apartment after her mom died. The poor woman suffered from hoarding and allowed no one except family members' access to her apartment for any reason. This was true for electricians and maintenance personnel, despite the fact that repairs were necessary. One of the bathrooms in the two-bathroom apartment could not be used because of all the stored clutter in the bathtub, sink, and on top of the toilet bowl. Cabinets and closets were already filled to capacity, containing bottles of horse and dog shampoo, although she owned neither a horse nor a dog. Objects covered most of the floor and there was just a narrow walkway from the entrance to the back of the apartment. Clothes that did not fit her or had never been worn, were packed into closets along with about 110 pairs of shoes, 100+ scarves, and about 150 belts. Endless "To Do" checklists, written on the backs of used envelopes, were saved. Two out of the three bedrooms could not be used, since they were filled to capacity with "stuff."

After having suffered from so many fears myself, I could truly empathize with the anxieties of this addled woman. I felt very sorry that she did not receive the help she deserved when she was alive.

2

Causes and Consequences of OCD

About thirty years ago, OCD sufferers had very little recourse. We were just labeled as "crazy," and were presumed to have an uncommon psychological illness that perhaps was caused by flaws in our upbringing. Because of the stigma, it was not surprising that many sufferers took great lengths to conceal their compulsions under a cloak of secrecy. In the last twenty years, however, the research has shown OCD to be quite common, occurring in about 2 or 3 percent of the population (Osborn, 5-6). In the United States of America, anywhere from four to six million people are suffering from this disease at any given time.

OCD is now considered to be what is called a "neurobiological" disease. New imaging techniques have made brain research possible and brains of OCD sufferers and their controls have been studied using several methods, one of which is positron emission tomography (PET). According to the web source University of Utah: Genetic Science Learning Center, "Brain Imaging Technologies," researchers give the subject a radioactive isotope (modified sugar, or glucose) by injection in a PET scan. When the positively charged particles from the modified glucose collide with negatively charged particles (electrons) in a person's brain, energy is given off. The PET scanner measures the energy and a computer turns the energy measurements into colorful images that can be interpreted. The areas of the brain that absorb more of the modified sugar show greater activity, with red images displaying high levels, and blue images exhibiting low levels.

Researchers Judith Rapoport and Susan Swedo at the National Institute of Mental Health, have found that the two areas of the brain that absorb the modified radioactive sugar and show a great deal of activity in OCD patients, compared to their controls, are the basal ganglia and the orbital frontal region. When OCD subjects are treated, the nerve firings in the basal ganglia and orbital frontal regions decrease and sometimes even vanish altogether. These findings now link the symptoms of OCD to the hyperactivity of nerves in these brain areas (Osborn, 180).

Chemical evidence for the biological basis of OCD comes from research studies that show a class of medications called the selective serotonin re-uptake inhibitors (SSRIs), also known as the anti-depressants, to be effective medications for the treatment of OCD. Serotonin is one of many neurotransmitters in the brain. The serotonin re-uptake inhibitors interfere with the absorption of serotonin. SSRI medications presumably exert their therapeutic effect by decreasing the nerve impulses, or firings, in the basal ganglia and orbital frontal circuit of the brain (Osborn, 94). Although OCD is associated with abnormal serotonin activity, much about this disorder is still not known. The cause of this disease is not as simple as too much or too little serotonin. Further investigations must be made in order for scientists to be able to explain the cause of this malady (Osborn, 182).

What impressed me most about OCD being a "biological brain disorder" was that my illness was not my own fault. Years ago, I was confronted with the fact that I had OCD by my own husband, who had observed my checking behaviors. I cried, denied it to the hilt, and refused to even discuss the possibility that I had such an illness. I felt my anxieties and rituals were due to a personal weakness and did not want the stigma of a mental disorder. The last thing I wanted to do was admit my own failures and faults to anyone, even the members of my own family.

Osborn likens OCD to coronary heart disease, whereby symptoms of an illness can be explained by observing biological processes. For example, the shortness of breath and chest pain caused by fatty tissue (plaque) that clogs the coronary arteries feeding the heart causes heart attacks. By the same token, the symptoms of OCD rituals and compulsions, can now be explained by "measurable chemical abnormalities that occur in specific regions of the brain" (178).

It is my personal opinion that the general public has yet to grasp this fact. When a woman in my neighborhood had a heart attack in her early fifties, she received a great deal of sympathy from her friends, neighbors, and employer. Flowers, food, and cards were sent. That is the way it should be when a person becomes ill. However, when I was hospitalized, it was clear that people did not understand the extent of this "biological illness." There was little acknowledgment by acquaintances and friends; instead, there was avoidance. There were few phone calls, saying, "How are you feeling?" My neighbor was given time to recover from her heart condition and return to work. My career was terminated. This was not necessarily because people lack compassion – rather because they just do NOT understand. Hopefully, as time goes by, the general population will become more educated about the biological basis of obsessive-compulsive disorder.

What Happens to Those of Us with OCD?

OCD causes real and intense suffering. You cannot "escape" your doubting mind. Although your fears might seem "silly" to an outsider who does not have OCD, they are certainly not silly to you. I was not aware that I was suffering from false guilt and false fear. During one particularly severe bout, my appetite decreased significantly, and I dropped from 120 to 107 pounds in about 3 months. I was terrorized by unrelenting negative thoughts, and my concentration was significantly impaired. I endured many nights with little or no sleep, and as a result, ended up developing sleep anxiety, whereby I became very anxious about my inability to fall asleep at night. For a while, my fears about not sleeping not only kept me awake, but then morphed into another fear about getting into a car, falling asleep at the wheel and severely harming someone else. My anxiety became chronic and I became overly preoccupied with the fear of not sleeping for a substantial part of the day. I also developed anxiety's bed partner, depression, which one third of all OCD sufferers experience as well. I was eventually hospitalized because I asked my uncle to help me end my life. Living with OCD was like living in a mental prison.

OCD creates so much doubt, that you begin to believe you are not a good person despite evidence to the contrary. Personality profiles of typical OCD sufferers have shown that they suffer from exaggerated responsibility. Intrinsically, we are commonly very decent, morally upright people. Unfortunately, many times that is not the way we see ourselves. I was very critical, self-condemning, and convinced that I was responsible for a variety of possible catastrophic scenarios that involved harming either myself or others. I doubted my ability to do my job as a teacher despite good evaluations, to take care of my real responsibilities at home (which I always had), to drive safely (despite a good driving record), and to relate to people in a non-offensive way, despite the fact that my intention is to be a generally pleasant person. OCD tells you, "You are no good. You may have hurt someone." This is a symptom of the illness. I remember my dear Uncle Joey telling me hundreds of times, "You are a really good person," in an effort to help me overcome my tremendous self-doubt. It took me a long while to start believing it.

    OCD also diminished my sense of perspective. In the midst of OCD thinking, I would become preoccupied with the minutia of a task and forget the big picture. For example, I became preoccupied with an attendance error I made once in marking a student absent when she actually came in late. I felt incredibly guilty for days on end and overlooked the fact that I was competent and dedicated in the basic aspect of the job – teaching. True, I made an error but it was of no great significance. This is an illustration of making mountains out of molehills – a behavior that made my life significantly worse.

    OCD dashes hopes and dreams, preventing you from achieving your true potential. Although I graduated college magna cum laude as a science major, took both the dental and law boards and scored very well, fear, intolerance of uncertainty, and the lack of confidence due to continual self-doubt kept me from pursuing many aspirations. Obsessive-compulsive disorder clouds your thinking to the point where you might not know where your responsibility ends and where someone else's begins. The attribute of taking on much more responsibility than necessary feeds OCD. This was one of my major weaknesses in which I needed a great deal of help, and so I devoted an entire chapter (7) to this subject.

Most importantly, OCD interferes with happiness, functioning, and productivity. I was not as productive as I could have been, while wasting a great deal of time checking. I certainly was not happy, surviving with guilt and fear. At my worst point, I was alive, but not really "living." I became very self-absorbed and withdrawn, expending tremendous energy on reducing anxiety by avoiding feared situations, feeling guilty and miserable all the while. That, in turn, diminished the more loving relationships I could have had with family members, friends, and with the community at large.

The good news is that there is a great sense of optimism about OCD recovery, more so now than ever before. There are presently two "standard" treatments for this illness, cognitive behavior therapy, and the SSRI medications. Yet, medication and cognitive therapy are not the entire story. How medications actually work is not well understood. There are people that have been given both treatments and still have not been released from the powerful grip of obsessive-compulsive disorder.

I believe that spirituality, the belief in God, and His power within you, should be a big (and perhaps the most important) part of this healing equation. I have experienced firsthand what a spiritual belief system with a whole new set of values accomplished toward my recovery. I would like to share it with anyone that is tortured by obsessive-compulsive disorder, so that he or she may find relief from the burdens of this illness, and experience a rebirth (as I have), where peace has largely replaced anxiety.

3

My Personal Spiritual Journey

There is no question that I underwent quite a remarkable spiritual journey in my life. I wish to share this experience so that there is clarity about my definition of spirituality, which is basically the love of all humankind.

I grew up in a Christian home. My parents were of German descent, born Lutheran. My mother regularly attended a Lutheran church in our neighborhood for many years. Although my father lived with us until his death in 1967, I never remember him attending any religious service. My introduction to church, and my subsequent attendance, confirmation and church wedding were really driven by my mother.

My first memorable church experience was when I was about six or seven years old in Sunday school. I remember being told that if people did not believe in and obey God, they would go to hell. "Going to heaven" was the reward for those people who did believe. I asked my teacher what hell was like, and was told that it was a place where "bad" people go to be eternally punished by burning. A little confused, I asked her if I could "feel" fire after death. She replied, "Oh yes, you can feel it just as you would feel a burn on your finger." So, I developed a mindset that hell was a place of torture – a place to be avoided at all costs. Being a fearful child to begin with, this conversation had a lasting impression on me, since for a long time, I believed that one went to church and performed good deeds in order to avoid hell and to insure a good after-life in heaven.

At the age of about twelve, our church required mandatory attendance at both confirmation class and church services. Again, the most memorable lessons were the ones from the pastor issuing stern warnings about judgment after death; I was going to be put on some sort of cosmic scale, where good deeds would be weighed against bad ones, and I would be going to one of two places. It is interesting that my pastor told me that God was going to hold me accountable for every church service I missed. At that time in my life, I never speculated about his potential motives, taking his words quite literally. So, I went to church, trying to tip the scale of eternal judgment into the plus column, in order to soothe an angry God and avoid eternal damnation. Before the time of my actual confirmation, my father died, leaving my mother in emotionally and economically difficult circumstances. My presiding pastor was really not supportive (or even nice) to her at that time, and this led to some questions and criticisms of the church on my part. Yet, I still continued to attend out of fear.

My Personal Spiritual Journey

One fateful day, my "fire and brimstone" minister retired and was subsequently replaced – with a kinder and gentler married fellow. It was not long, however, until word was out in the congregation that he was getting divorced. Gossip was rampant, and our minister left, leaving me with the thought that ministers could fall off the moral pedestal and were perhaps just as sinful (and human) as the rest of us. He was, in turn, replaced by another compassionate man, who led Bible studies, was extremely approachable, and actually invited discourse.

One day, I asked him my pressing question: "What does one need to do in order to earn eternal salvation?" He replied, "All you have to do is believe that Jesus Christ is the Son of God." That response was very plain, simple, easy to understand and completely doable on my part. His belief was that everyone fell short according to God's standards, but we were all saved by grace, as long as we believed in Jesus Christ, the Son of God. It did not take me long to figure out that if all I had to do to achieve salvation was "believe," church attendance was no longer mandatory. Neither were good deeds, or concern for anyone else. I could do what I wanted, believe one simple statement, and I was part of the "club." So, I no longer feared God, and became very unconcerned with the whole issue of religion, (or spirituality) since, in my mind, the goal of achieving eternal life in heaven was a "done deal." I did not step inside a church, except to marry for the next twenty plus years. Of course, in hindsight, my spiritual development was very immature. I merely responded to a "carrot on a stick" model, thinking that the entire point of going to church and believing Christian principles was to achieve salvation, or in Christian terms, become "saved."

My interest in religion did not re-surface until I started to experience OCD symptoms. At this point, I began to have serious spiritual conversations with my Uncle Joey, after confiding in him that I was suffering from anxiety, depression and checking compulsions.

My uncle was an extremely interesting person and I must digress to share a little information about him. Joey was born Catholic, never attended church mass, yet he was the most loving person I have ever met. He was kind and compassionate to everyone, regardless of ethnicity, gender, religion, etc. and would never discriminate against anyone, although discriminatory practices were very common during his lifetime. His house was a revolving door for ailing relatives, whom his family took in and cared for. He was not a very wealthy person, yet he donated quite a large percentage of his money to charity and was known to respond to strangers' needs spontaneously. (He once met a barefoot woman on the street and took her to a shoe store to buy her shoes.) He had quite a reputation in his neighborhood as a helpful person, and strangers would ring his doorbell for help and inspiration. I called him many times at three or four in the morning when I was anxiety-ridden and needed spiritual comfort. My calls were always met with compassion, never anger, for calling (and probably disturbing) him in the middle of the night.

Joey was a progressive thinker and believed in equal rights for women even though he was born just before women achieved the right to vote. He was highly critical of injustice, inequality, and poverty and insisted on the fair treatment of all people. Joey was an advocate for the marginalized, sick and emotionally disturbed. He believed that a great deal of criminal behavior could be attributed to mental illness. (There is now neuro-scientific evidence that imprisoned criminals exhibit different brain patterns than the non-criminal population (Moskowitz).)

Joey's powers of observation were extraordinary, scientific and accurate. One time, we were sitting on a boardwalk bench and he spotted a set of keys at its end. When we were ready to leave, Joey suggested leaving the keys on the bench, thinking that the owner might return to our location, looking for them. While we were walking down the boardwalk, Joey spotted a man amongst many people walking in our opposing direction. He went up to the man and said, "Your keys are still on the bench." Both the man and I were astounded, since that same man did in fact lose his keys. How was Joey able to identify the man, a total stranger, who had lost his keys, so precisely? Joey told me that he was able to observe the worried look on his face. Fortunately, when I had a major problem with depression and OCD, Joey was there to observe my actions, perceive what I was going through emotionally, and made great (and successful) attempts to help me.

Joey thought an introduction to spirituality would heal my poor mental state. He introduced me to an interpretation of God that I had never known. Joey sincerely believed we are ALL God's children, and he treated ALL people regardless of race, gender, religion, physical differences, etc. as such. He told me that God was love. Period. There were no favorites. To have a relationship with God, and to really commune with God meant that I had to love everyone. My prejudices had to go. So, did anger, greed, pride, self-centeredness, jealousy, racism, sexism, violence, materialism, harsh words and negative thoughts.

Joey did not identify with religion in particular. He saw the Christian Bible as an allegoric book, with certain contradictions, rather than the complete, inerrant word of God. In fact, he believed that he was inspired by God over time, to own his spiritual belief system, and that God could inspire each and every one of us. The idea that I, myself, could be inspired by God was at first ludicrous, but became acceptable, and finally convincing.

Having said that, however, there are wonderful passages in the Bible containing profound words of wisdom that Joey emphasized, and that I came to believe in and attempt to practice on a daily basis. In the *New Testament of the Bible, Matthew 22:37-40*, we are given two commandments. The first is that "ye shall love the Lord your God with all your heart, with all your soul, and with all your mind." This is the first and greatest commandment. And the second is: "You shall love your neighbor as yourself. On these two commandments hang all the Law and the Prophets." These passages are basically the summation of the entire New Testament, and what I believe to be the essence of ALL religions. In fact, all religions do have some version of the "golden rule" – we do unto others, as we want others to do unto us.

Examples of various "golden rule" versions can be found at **religioustolerance.org**, in the following religious texts:

- Judaism: "...thou shalt love thy neighbor as thyself." Leviticus 19:18.
- Islam: "None of you [truly] believes until he wishes for his brother what he wishes for himself." Number 13 of Imam "Al-Nawawi's Forty Hadiths."
- Christianity: "And as ye would that men should do to you, do ye also to them likewise." Luke 6:31,

King James Version.
- Buddhism: "Hurt not others in ways that you yourself would find hurtful." Udana-Varga 5:18.
- Hinduism: "This is the sum of duty: do not do to others what would cause pain if done to you." Mahabharata 5:1517.
- Confucianism: "Do not do to others what you do not want them to do to you." Analects 15:23.

The concept of the golden rule, caring for others as you care for yourself, is universal. I believe a person must really strive to live by it if one is to become spiritual. I specifically use the term "spiritual," rather than "religious" because there are distinctions. My understanding of spirituality is that it can include religion but recognizes that we are all part of one whole, regardless of culture, ethnicity, gender, race, and religion. Religion is based on a clear set of rules, or doctrine, while spirituality does not endorse a specific ideology. Many religions claim to have the truth, whereas spirituality recognizes that there are many paths to the Divine. Above all, spirituality is based on love, not fear, and encourages us to unify, rather than to divide. It also focuses on discovering God within ourselves, which can be immensely powerful in promoting love, peace and understanding in our world.

There will be several occasions in this book when I

will make references to the Bible, as opposed to other spiritual literature. This is because I grew up with a Christian background and this particular scripture is now what I am most familiar with. I also think there are biblical passages that are extremely important for all of us to know about and to practice. These verses have helped me immeasurably in my life and I sincerely believe that they can help everyone, Christians and non-Christians alike.

For example, there is a short line in the Christian Bible that left an indelible impression and it basically says, "in order to gain life, you must lose it." It took me years to understand what this line meant. Now, I interpret it to mean that spirituality means dying an ego death. For a major portion of my life, every event was considered from my perspective only, with only a minimal regard for the perspectives of others. When considering possible alternatives while confronting a given scenario, my thought life primarily consisted of questions such as: "How will this benefit me? What have I got to lose? How do I feel about this? How will this affect my future?" When pondering the future, I usually projected negative outcomes, and then would proceed to avoid them at all costs.

When I adopted spirituality, my thought life was altered to consider the perspectives of others as well as my own. Questions such as: "How will my actions and speech affect others? How am I making someone else feel? What if

I compete and I lose? If I lose, another person will gain. Is that so bad?" The answer is "no." My life is not only about me. I must become the master of myself so that I can be a servant to others (a favorite line of my memorable minister).

During periods of my life, I had a continual worry about what would happen to me in the future. What if something bad happened? What if I got sick? What if I did not make enough money? What if .... (fill in the blank with any negative possibility). As I adopted spirituality, my worries about myself radically diminished. I began to think in the following way, "I am a child of God, like everyone else in this world. Adversity is a part of life. Everyone has his or her share. Am I so important that I need to worry about myself? The answer is 'not really.' At some point in everyone's life there is demise. The world will go on without me. I have lived a good life with few regrets. God is good to me. I would like to reciprocate and be good to His children."

Unfortunately, for a long while, I was obsessed with the Christian idea of salvation, not just for myself, but also for my friends and loved ones. The very idea of eternal reward and punishment caused me a great deal of pain and inner conflict to the point where I became suicidal. I was actually told by a fundamental Christian that if I believed and spoke about the idea that we are all God's children that

My Personal Spiritual Journey

I would end up in hell myself. However, my dear uncle intervened, and spoke about a God who loved everyone. He supported the universalist idea of salvation for all, (although this is not a mainstream Protestant view.) I also started reading some more literature, such as Pastor Rob Bell's, *Love Wins*, where he supports a universalist view, stating that it's a terrible contradiction for a loving God to torture "non-believers" forever. Equally important, is his opinion that we should be working toward a heaven here on earth, free of war, greed, injustice, rape, poverty and murder. He writes, "Often the people most concerned about others going to hell when they die seem less concerned with the hells on earth right now, while the people most concerned with the hells on earth right now seem the least concerned about hell after death." (78-79).

    I am painfully well aware that to some conservative Christian groups, the belief that Jesus Christ is the literal Son of God, is mandatory for salvation. When comparing the great religions of the world, one will find that conservative Islamic groups insist that belief in Allah and the Koran is essential for salvation. Some Jewish groups do not believe in a hell but believe in a heaven. Buddhist beliefs suggest that both heaven and hell can exist right here on this earth. Sikhism proposes that individuals who commit sufficient good works are released from a cycle of reincarnation and are joined with God. Some Mormons believe in multiple heavens, while many atheists believe in no heaven at all. Universalists, who believe that everyone goes to heaven, have made a case for a heaven but no hell. I had counseling from a pastor who believed that there is a hell, but it was largely empty, compared with heaven.

As far as the Christian Bible is concerned, there are verses that support both a Universalist and a judgment point of view. For the Christians that support judgment, different criteria for entering paradise are proposed – some insist that faith alone is sufficient for salvation, while others believe that good works are necessary. Just by doing a little research one can find not only different opinions about the afterlife between religions; one can find enormous differences of opinions between people professing to be part of the same religion.

My own research, powers of logic and thoughtful conversations with my uncle allow me to make two comments about all of this. First of all, if we start off with the premise that "God is Love" *("1 John 4: 8:* Whoever does not love does not know God, for God is Love") then the idea of a God who eternally damns one of his children is a very apparent contradiction. What kind of God would punish his children forever? How could God commit such an evil act when he is a God of Love?

My second comment is that there is a great deal of debate about an afterlife. There are many, many differing opinions on whether there is an afterlife, a heaven, hell, and the criteria required to enter either place. There is just no common script for all of us to follow.

I pondered why there are so many conflicting opinions. It is a very human and unfortunately, egotistical desire to want to live forever. I have come to terms with the uncertainty that I don't know what happens after death. I personally am not convinced that anyone really knows for sure. That is okay. I have learned to live with this uncertainty. My best educated guess is that we ought to lead lives trying to do good whenever possible.

My previous next-door neighbor, Judy F., is extraordinarily helpful and genuinely kind to everyone she meets; she is a loving person who makes friends and establishes a positive rapport with people regardless of age, gender, and race quite easily. I once asked her if she expected anything in return for all the good she had done for me during my life. She responded, "I lead a life of goodness not because of some end reward; having done good IS the reward." I learned a profound life lesson from her that day. When I now attempt to help others, I do not expect reciprocity. I am already rewarded because God has enabled me to die an ego death in order to help others.

My spiritual journey has taken me from a reward and punishment model living with fear and suffering, to a new place, where my life is dedicated to doing good here on earth. That means showing compassion, forgiveness, mercy, humility, tolerance, generosity, justice, nobility and grace for all those I come into contact with – the very qualities that God exemplifies. Rather than worrying about salvation, I feel that I should be more concerned about fighting poverty, inequality and injustice while here on earth. I have found that allowing God to rule my life, both in thought and in deed, and doing what I think pleases my Creator, has led me to inner peace and a sense of purpose. **Let us all partner with God and try to create a little heaven here on earth.**

4

Believe in God's Healing Power Within You

The idea that spirituality can aid in mental health healing does have support in published literature. I found a book by Dr. Ian Osborn entitled, *Can Christianity Cure OCD?* The title of this book intrigued me. Dr. Osborne describes the biographies of Martin Luther (1483–1546), founder of Lutheranism, Paul Bunyan (1628–1688), pastor and author of *The Pilgrim's Progress*, and the Catholic Saint Therese (1873-1897). Each of these famous Christian figures was an OCD sufferer, and each was released from their torment. Luther and Bunyan were saved by their faith and trust in Christ (89), while St. Therese developed and benefited from her philosophy of "absolute surrender to God" (107). These great theologians found that practicing spirituality was a successful healing tool in the past, when there was no medication, no cognitive behavioral therapy, and OCD was not yet labeled as a neurobiological mental illness.

When I was ill, I wanted to get well and function again more than anything else and was ready to devote my heart, mind and soul to that endeavor. I now firmly believe that my faith and spirituality have helped me enormously, in part by getting me to focus more on others as opposed to myself. Today, I think about, talk and pray to God on a regular basis. I believe God has been my ultimate healer. Living and thinking spiritually is an exemplary medicine for attaining peace and overcoming anxiety. It has worked for me, and it can work for you. It was not easy to become spiritual and reject many of the earthly values (such as materialism, one-upmanship) that I learned and practiced over the course of my entire life. It took effort to develop the faith that has made me feel well, but it was well worth it.

In the *New Testament, Luke (8:43–48)*, a story is told about a woman who was hemorrhaging for twelve years and comes from behind Jesus in a crowd to touch his cloak. Jesus calls out to the crowd, and asks, "Who touched me?" The trembling woman steps forward and admits to the entire crowd how it was she who touched him and was healed immediately. Jesus says to her, "Daughter, your faith has made you well. Go in peace." A cure is her reward for her faith. If we exercise enough faith, we too can be healed. I am a modern-day example of someone whose faith has helped them heal, just as that hemorrhaging woman. I practice putting my faith in God, touching His metaphorical cloak when necessary. Faith needs to be developed and nurtured over time and with enough dedication, it will increase as you practice.

For our own benefit, we must try to exercise our God-given ability of faith instead of doubt. Your faith can be nurtured in many ways – by prayer, meditation, associating with spiritual people, reading spiritual literature, attending spiritual places of worship, and so on.

An Argument for the Existence of a Supreme Being

When I was much younger, I questioned the existence of God. As a young adult, I became a science teacher, and was impressed by the facts, laws, and theories presented by the scientific community. As I matured, I also remember being impressed by the beauty and the miracles of nature, easily observable in my uncle's garden. I enjoyed watching the many different plants - tomatoes, figs, grapes, lilacs, roses, and evergreen trees - growing and thriving there, inspiring me to eventually create a garden of my own. I visited many of the United States National Parks, and began to appreciate the earth's biodiversity even more, learning how interconnected and interdependent all living things really are. The fact that animals depend on photosynthetic plants and algae for their food while scavengers and decomposers recycle their remains into reusable chemical components, profoundly impressed me. Essential elements and compounds, such as carbon, nitrogen and water, required for biological life, are continuously recycled. Who could have created such perfect systems where essential materials are reprocessed over and over? Was this incredible web of life a pure coincidence, or was there a creator responsible for all life?

As a student, I gave little thought to how our universe and life began, other than believing in the Darwinian theory of natural selection (how traits of organisms within a species vary, giving some individuals a reproductive advantage, and how populations ultimately change over time giving rise to new species), and his theory of evolution, which states that all organisms on this planet have descended from a common ancestor. However, at one point, life must have begun from something non-living. This process, called spontaneous generation, according to scientists, must have occurred ONCE to explain the origin of life. If we are to accept that life occurred from something non-living, then why is this process NOT ongoing? Why can no one duplicate spontaneous generation in a test tube? Again, I thought: did our wonderfully designed universe have a designer?

Let us suppose that you are walking along a road and you find a bunch of coins scattered about. How did they get there? A likely explanation would be that someone was walking along, and perhaps had a perforated pocket that contained spare change. It is likely that the change fell out of the pocket in a random pattern. So, one might assume that the coins got there by accident. But suppose, however, that you are walking along the same road, and you see the coins stacked in nice, neat, orderly piles of pennies, nickels, dimes and quarters. How did they get there? Now, the idea that they got there by accident is much less plausible. It would be perfectly reasonable to assume that the coins were intentionally ordered.

We can extrapolate this analogy to our universe. The order of our own solar system is very observable: the moon revolves around the earth, and the planets and their moons revolve around the sun in a very mathematically predictable fashion. How was this order created?

Was it by some random accident or does the universe have a Master Designer with a divine plan? I personally believe that the universe, which has more stars than the earth has grains of sand, is too complex, majestic and organized to have occurred by mere chance. I feel that there must be a higher power that is intentionally responsible for all creation. For me, this Supreme Being is our creator, God.

Every one of us has a deep spiritual need in our life. Evidence for this premise is the fact that religious behavior has been, and still is exhibited in every area of the world. It has also existed in every stage of development in human history. The ability to have faith in a superior being is hardwired into our neural circuitry (Wade). We benefit enormously when we exercise our need to be spiritual.

How can We Describe our Supreme Being?

Simply put, I believe that the Supreme Being is our creator and healer, and who loves all of us unconditionally. This Supreme Being exemplifies kindness, compassion, forgiveness, mercy, justice, grace, and all things good. This is my definition of God. God is love. The spirit of God also resides in all of us. This is my view as well as the view of many other spiritual people.

Beautiful words in the *New Testament of the Bible, (Romans 8:38)*, written by the Apostle Paul which had a significant impact on me are:

> "For I am persuaded that neither death nor life, nor angels nor principalities nor powers, nor things present nor things to come, nor height nor depth, nor any other created thing, shall be able to separate us from the love of God which is in Jesus Christ our Lord."

Paul was a person who underwent a deep spiritual conversion. He was totally transformed from a persecutor of Christians to one of the great writers of the New Testament. Such a spiritual conversion is worth mentioning because it is not unusual. It happened to Paul, and to me, and it can happen to you. Paul wants the world to know that God's love is forever. No one can separate us from it other than ourselves. We need to acknowledge this love, treasure and share it.

Whenever I refer to the "Supreme Being," creator, or the "Divine Being" in this book, the pronoun "He" will be used out of convenience, although I do not believe that God is necessarily a being that has any particular gender or form. In traditional Christianity, there is an emphasis on the Trinity, that is the Father (God), son (Jesus Christ) and the Holy Spirit (the divine within). I personally believe everyone has the Divine within – a powerful (and good) force that we can exercise – as long as we believe it is there. It is precisely because I think everyone has God within them, that I see all people as children of God, whether they share my belief systems or not.

Dr. Michael Murray N.D., author of, *What the Drug Companies Won't Tell You and Your Doctor Doesn't Know*, indicates that your very own body is an amazing healing machine. Notice how your blood clots when your skin is pierced and you start bleeding. God gave you a body with a spontaneous capability to heal itself. We all have His divine healing power within us and can call upon it at any time. Love, patience, kindness, faithfulness, and the ability to heal reside in the inner sanctuary of each and every one of us. God can help us overcome the problems in our lives when we exercise our faith. I call upon you, dear reader, to call upon God, your higher power, or whatever Supreme Being you believe in, to help you during adverse conditions.

Because God is love, I believe that God's plan for us is good. He wants us to have serenity and accept his continual offer of peace. When we give our troubles to God, He replaces it with His peace. Because God is love, He is forgiving. Because God loves us unconditionally, He is so merciful that he loves and accepts us in spite of our faults.

If we allow our human nature to dictate the course of our life, we can expect conflict, stress, anxiety and dissatisfaction. Earthly desire for possessions, lust, or the yearning for power or control, just lead to a never-ending cycle of wanting more (whatever that may be for you), but spiritual desire results in true fulfillment that we all ultimately seek. These words of wisdom are also pointed out in *Romans 8, Verse 6* where it says, "To be controlled by human nature results in death; to be controlled by the Spirit results in life and peace." A life dedicated to doing good for our Divine Being results in peace, a sense of purpose and a meaningful life.

What is the Purpose of Adversity in our Lives?

It seems that all people undergo trials and

tribulations, and suffering is part of life. I have often asked myself, "Why does God allow this?" There are several philosophical reasons. If things went continuously well, we would never learn to appreciate our blessings, since we would have no basis of comparison. Perhaps one reason we suffer is to learn to value all the blessings we already have.

In Dr. Stanley's book, *How to Handle Adversity*, he proposes that "There is a divine purpose behind all adversity" (156). Suffering directs us to be dependent on God and builds character, compassion and spiritual maturity (97). Stanley stated that he learned his greatest life lessons during prolonged adversity (127). I believe there is quite a bit of merit to this argument.

With God All Things are Possible

When you come to the end of your rope and admit defeat, then you are ready to entrust your life and your future to your higher power. When you realize you cannot stand on your own, you are then ready to allow God to be the center of your life, and a healing and loving relationship begins (152). God's sustaining healing power sees us through any trial we may face.

Spirituality has the power to transform your entire life. Your body is already a miracle. God's healing power is greater than any illness. God has NO limitations. If you have gotten the idea that your OCD cannot be helped, DO NOT believe it; that is just another OCD falsehood and part of the illness. In addition, in the *New Testament, Matthew 19:26*, it states that "With men this is impossible, but with God all things are possible." I encourage you, dear reader, to firmly believe this.

Can spirituality help cure OCD? My answer is a resounding, "yes." It was successful in the past, it is successful today, and it will be successful in the future. Know your true identity and develop a relationship with the Supreme Being. Once you recognize the divine within you, and develop a loving relationship with Him, your battles with obsessive-compulsive disorder will be enormously easier. And the more you focus on your higher power, and doing good for all of God's children, the better you will feel. Realize that we all are on a spiritual journey, and our most noble ultimate goal is a loving relationship with a divine being, as well as with our earthly brothers and sisters.

5

Dealing with Legalism and Perfectionism

Many people with OCD (including me) have a compulsion to ensure that everything is absolutely perfect. My "perfectionism" took the following forms when I tried to:

- Say things exactly right, so that no one could possibly be offended.
- Make sure I read and comprehended something flawlessly.
- Follow religious doctrines and rules of employment perfectly.
- Follow the letter of every law to the "nth" degree both on my job, and in completing tasks that involved money.
- Create a home environment that was "perfectly safe" for my children.

When I taught science and final grading time came around, I checked and re-checked the grades many times for fear of a transposing an error from my own grade sheet to the master school list (before the widespread use of digital software). I spent hours developing complex formulas to ascertain grades, and when they were entered on a final computerized sheet, I would have my husband read them aloud, while I checked the grades again.

I also worried when I created an exam and thought a student might have possibly somehow "seen" a question in advance. The student would then have had an unfair advantage over his classmates. I would endlessly revise exams to alleviate my doubt about this possibility.

When my children were small I became obsessed with keeping my home **perfectly** safe. It is normal for parents to want to protect their children, but looking back on things, I became inordinately (and irrationally) fearful. For example, I had a morbid fear of my children sticking their fingers into an electric pencil sharpener and thereby amputating them. Our house had a small laundry chute in a bathroom cabinet, and I begged my husband to seal it because I thought our children would climb in and fall down. (He did seal it somewhat to appease me, but he honestly thought that the width of the chute was smaller than the body of a child and that my fear was unwarranted.) I became fearful of pens (imagining they could poke their eyes out), plastic bags (they could place them over their heads and suffocate the minute I was not looking), washers/dryers (kids could crawl in the machines and turn them on), broken glass fragments (which could end up in food, and the digestive systems of my little ones). The list was endless. I envisioned ordinary household tools and appliances as grave threats after fabricating scenarios in which my children became injured. It took me a long time to understand that one hundred percent perfection and zero percent risk were unattainable.

It is my experience that worrying about every technicality can make you sick, and eventually leave you unable to function and do your job. My administrator wanted to make me a "model" teacher, so that my colleagues could observe some of my teaching techniques. She obviously was impressed with what she saw in the classroom. But I was oblivious to her confidence in me. I enjoyed my work but ended up leaving, because trying to follow every technicality perfectly, worrying about the accuracy of grades and test questions, the evaluations of administrators, and the prospect of unhappy parents and students eventually became overwhelming. Trying to have perfect lessons, assessments, paperwork and inordinate concerns about student safety also took its toll.

Dr. Fed Penzel, an OCD therapist, once said, "If a policeman were to follow every single rule, he would not be able to do his job." I know from personal experience that this is unfortunately true. Although I was perceived as a competent professional I eventually could not function on the job and left, which did not benefit my family, my students, or me.

I had an urge to confess many trivial things that I "may" have done wrong during my illness, and for a long time, refused to acknowledge that I suffered from extreme legalism although my Uncle Joey affirmed that I had this problem. In hindsight, I am now aware of my many unnecessary attempts to follow man-made rules to the exact letter of the law. Some examples of my adherence to legalism are as follows:

- Every single rule in my work environment had to be adhered to. And there were plenty of rules.
- I tried to understand and follow every rule of tax law when completing my tax forms. When the value of something, like damage to my property from a hurricane, or donations of books and used clothing was not exactly concrete, calculating a subjective value caused me enormous stress. I frustrated very competent accountants!
- I tried to follow religious doctrine perfectly and felt enormous guilt when I failed, particularly when it came to church donations.

I also remember when I started to win my battle with legalism after acknowledging that I had this problem. One time, I went Christmas shopping with my husband and daughters at an outlet center. The girls needed a few gifts for friends as well as for each other. The shopping center publishes a coupon book, which we brought along. My oldest daughter saw a pair of high-heeled boots that she wanted. I thought that they were highly impractical, but my younger child wanted to please her sister, and encouraged me to purchase them anyway. I had found a 15% coupon from the booklet so I decided to acquiesce to my daughter's wishes and stood in line to pay for the boots while the girls continued to shop. When I got to the cashier, she examined the coupon and refused to accept it because the cost of the boots fell below a stipulated price of $75. I examined the coupon thoroughly and saw there was no minimum purchase specified. I then asked her how she came up with the "minimum purchase price," and she said that she did not come up with anything – her manager came up with the limit. I answered by saying that the minimum price must be stated on the coupon, and if it was not in writing, then the manager's limit should not be applicable. The cashier became so annoyed with my persistence that she just rang up the boots with a 15% discount. I walked out of the store, and instead of feeling victorious, I felt guilty and doubtful. Suppose I had misread the coupon? Shouldn't I have discussed the matter with the appropriate manager? Suppose I had cheated the store somehow? I began to persecute myself all the way home.

I considered going back to the store the following day to return the boots, just to spare myself the "guilt." However, my new spiritual awareness began to kick in, and I began to talk to myself differently. Even though I felt doubt about my accuracy in reading the coupon, I realized that in the worst-case scenario I made a mistake. I was entitled to make errors; God forgives us for them. I knew that I would never intentionally cheat anyone. Therefore, knowing God's forgiveness, I felt peace come over me, and no longer stressed about the boots. I knew God would never condemn me, and He did NOT want me to condemn myself. This was the beginning of a change in my way of thinking. I did not return the boots, and I remember this incident as being the first step in overcoming my legalistic thinking.

I realize that to many readers, this is a rather trivial incident when one could consider a broad range of sins one could commit. Many of my worries were, in fact, inconsequential, however, I did not have this awareness. I was an expert at making mountains out of molehills and did not distinguish major transgressions from very minor ones, causing myself much needless suffering. In addition, I wasted a lot of time worrying about tiny details, and being extraordinarily guilt-prone, while losing a big picture perspective of the world around me.

A word should be mentioned here about religious

scrupulosity, a common form of OCD in which sufferers have irrational, unwanted thoughts and/or fears about not being pious enough, or not following religious laws or man-made laws perfectly. Sufferers are excessively concerned about sinning against God by having "immoral thoughts" or disappointing Him in some way. A devout person is tormented by doubt about his goodness, despite the fact that he is a highly moral person. To reduce anxiety, a scrupulous person might repeat prayers, phrases or perform acts of penance excessively. Even after much time is spent praying, or ritualizing, the person may feel that he or she did not pray adequately (Nelson, Abramowitz, Whiteside and Deacon, 2006).

Researcher Stephen Phillipson (2006) suggests that sufferers of religious scrupulosity feel their behavior is displeasing to God and feel intense guilt and anxiety as a result. To relieve the anxiety, many engage in repetitive prayer or religious rituals at the expense of developing a loving relationship with God. What is of foremost importance is that we have a true relationship with God, NOT that we follow every rule to the "nth" degree. When we connect with God, we can throw our mental list of "do's and don'ts" in the garbage can. Gone is the anxiety and stress about following the rules. God knows our heart's intent and the circumstances. He is not a stern master who is ready to punish us if we don't follow the rules, and we do NOT need to punish ourselves.

There is a fundamental difference between a scrupulous and a spiritual person. While the scrupulous person is excessively concerned with following the tenets of religion, repeating religious rituals or prayers over and over, she derives no pleasure from them. She may follow the rules down to the minutest level, but the big picture of spirituality, such as love and concern for others, is lost. The scrupulous individual is performing repetitive acts merely to relieve her irrational fears and anxieties. The compulsions bring temporary relief, but the distress returns fairly quickly, and with renewed intensity. A spiritually inspired person may also perform some religious rituals but he finds them rewarding. More importantly, he sees their value in perspective, and his heart is filled with peace (Phillipson).

I remember attending a church service once and learning about Christ's opposition to legalism. It was the first time I had really understood the term. Jesus was highly criticized at the time for violating the Sabbath law by the Pharisees, a religious group highly concerned with rules and regulations. Christ healed a man's hand on the Sabbath when it was supposed to be a day of rest. Jesus firmly defended Himself, saying, "it is lawful to do good on the Sabbath." He also called the Pharisees hypocrites, and accused them of unfairly laying heavy burdens upon men's shoulders, because they required people to follow trivial laws, but ignored faith, justice and mercy. He told the Pharisees that their traditions came from men, NOT from God. True spirituality came from a loving heart.

The reason that I am recounting this story is that there are many modern-day people that follow the letter of the law but, in fact, are blind to justice, kindness and compassion. One of the greatest "Pharisees" I have ever known was **me**. I was trying to follow the letter of the law to appease my guilt, not out of a heart of love, but from one of fear. It was the ensuing guilt I feared – guilt that would make me miserable. There was no evaluation of rules through a lens of justice or love, or critical thinking about why they existed. I was merely blindly trying to follow rules in ritualistic fashion, just because they were there.

I struggled for a long time to give up trying to follow the law to an infinitesimal degree. Legalism can be a very intrinsic part of the OCD illness. With God's gracious help, we can win this battle against legalism and direct our hearts toward following the beneficial **spirit** behind the law.

In my OCD days, I had no sense of perspective and was fixated on the possibility of making an error. I magnified a theoretical negative outcome about trivial incidents. As OCD sufferers, we tend not to let ourselves live life; we can be very self-incriminating. Until I eventually saw the big picture: that I was an intrinsically good and moral person trying to do the right thing, I suffered enormously. Secondly, I realized that God made us with the propensity to make mistakes, and we make them every day. As the saying goes, it is human to err, and divine to forgive. God wants us to forgive ourselves. It took me a long time to realize this. Growing up from a Christian perspective I was taught that we are sinners, and that we will sin again. However, I subsequently learned about God's grace. A dictionary definition of grace is "unmerited approval." *In Romans 6:14*, it says, "Sin shall not be master over you, for you are not under law, but under grace." God gives you His forgiveness. **You don't have to earn it by following a list of rules or doing deeds; it is freely given.** That is HOW GOOD God is to us. It is hard for us to imagine this because rarely do we meet humans that are so forgiving. God's love is so immense that His forgiveness has NO limits (Stanley, 83).

When I started to conjecture about what I may have done wrong, or inadequately, I began to speak to myself and say, "No matter what may have happened, or what I did, or may have done, the bottom line is that I am forgiven. Thank you, God, for your infinite mercy." After speaking to myself in this fashion, time after time, I slowly gave up trying to pursue perfectionism and consequently, am no longer anxious about making mistakes or fearing the ensuing guilt if things are not perfect.

I once went to church on All Saints Day, in which the Church commemorates all the saints, both recognized and unrecognized, and heard a sermon that had quite a positive impact on me. The minister asked us for a definition of a saint, and if we considered ourselves saints. I thought to myself, "Of course I am not a saint, since I am so very far from perfect." One church congregant brought up a very interesting point: St. Peter, who was one of the closest Disciples of Christ, actually denied knowing Christ when the guards arrested Him. Peter denied associating with Christ, not once, not twice, but three times, in order to save himself, when he was identified and questioned by the Roman authorities after realizing that Christ was in political trouble. He had human weaknesses just as we all do and showed a definite lack of courage when faced with the possibility of losing his life for his convictions. (I think that I would have reacted the same way as Peter – my fear would have prevailed under those challenging conditions.) Yet, he is still considered a "saint" not because he was perfect, but because of his dedication in spreading the Gospel. The minister actually suggested that the definition of a saint could be "anyone that has a loving, spiritual relationship with God and expresses that love to others." I subsequently became impressed with the fact that even the saints made mistakes and were flawed just like we are. If they were not perfect, then I did not have to be either. **Saints are ordinary people who are able to perform extraordinary feats.**

Another perspective is to think about perfection this way: to demand perfectionism from yourself, or anyone else for that matter, is very harsh. Trying to be perfect is a form of arrogance. Why do you have to do everything better than everyone else? Why set the bar so high for yourself, and then castigate yourself for not measuring up? Why not set the bar lower, and congratulate yourself when you have met or even exceeded the standard? I am capable of doing a greater amount of good for everyone for the long term if I don't have added stress of trying to be impossibly perfect. It is human (and normal) to err. If we practice self-reflection, we can also learn a lot from our mistakes, and try to improve our actions in future attempts.

Why would you want to be severe with yourself when you have such a loving, forgiving God? God accepts mediocrity. He does not expect perfection. If He wanted perfection, he would have made us perfect. No matter what we do, or don't do, we cannot disappoint Him. The more I would talk to myself about God and His standards, the more I was able to give up my own.

Let us also redefine the word "success." What is it

in your eyes? We grow up in a society where success can be defined by how much money we earn or what we acquire, the clothes we wear, the careers we choose, the extent of our sphere of influence, and so on. People struggle to get to the top of the ladder, to buy beautiful homes, automobiles, jewelry, stocks, bonds, and possessions of every type, only to find that these things do not bring lasting happiness or peace. Look at the current day pop stars and athletes with the fame and money they accumulate. When you look at the drug addiction and behavior of some, you can conclude that they are obviously not happy or peaceful. God's standards of "success" are very different than those of our American culture. If we are to adopt God's definition of success, then we need a reversal of values. Money or acquisitions cannot be our yardstick for achievement. God does not care about our status or what we acquire. God loves us because we are His creation. We can measure our success by the peace, gratitude and love we have in our hearts.

What then, are God's standards for us? God is not concerned with our pursuit of super-accuracy, perfection, or following the letter of the Law. God is already telling us, "I love you. Try to obey my wishes. My wish for you is to express what I represent, which is love. Try to be an expression of my love every waking moment. If you err, it is only a mistake; it does not diminish my love for you.

Please go forth and try again."

God wants us to focus on Him, instead of ourselves, and nurture our spiritual lives. We can achieve this by:

- Letting Him work through us and allowing ourselves to be an expression of His love and peace.
- Maintaining a good thought process and communicating with Him.
- Creating and striving for noble goals that help humanity.
- Appreciating all the blessings God has given us.

6

Dealing with the Guilt Accompanying OCD

Guilt is another cornerstone emotion of obsessive-compulsive disorder. It seems that we experience guilt for things that most people would not feel at all guilty about. In fact, guilt is usually the driving force that fuels the rituals. Sufferers fear that if "something were to happen, they might not be able to deal with the guilt."

I remember feeling guilty over many inactions. For example, my husband and I were driving to the airport, rushing because my flight left at 8 pm, and we were running somewhat late. On our way, I noticed a car had stopped in front of us, right before the intersection. When the light turned green, my husband drove around it, and I saw a man inside the car, with his head to one side. He appeared to me as if he were sleeping. My husband drove off without getting out of the car to see if the man was OK. I felt so guilty that I did not "force" my husband to stop our car – so I could check why this man left his car stationary, in a location with a high volume of traffic. Of course, my mind concocted a worst–case scenario! I thought to myself, "what if this man was having a heart attack and needed medical intervention? How could I have not stopped? So what if I had missed my flight?" I obsessed about this man on the way to the airport, on the plane, and for several days in my new destination, thinking this man might have died and it would be all my fault! (Of course, the idea that this man was having a heart attack was all conjecture!) Yet, my guilt was very severe and torturous – so much so that it overwhelmed me physically and mentally, causing me to feel worthless and ill. I could actually "feel" the churning in my abdomen.

I have felt very guilty about many other things in my lifetime. I remember feeling terribly guilty about touching another car's bumper at 5 to 10 mph, while trying to park in a tight New York City space. I would routinely check the bumpers of other cars over and over to reassure myself that I had not caused any damage. My reasoning was that if I were to do any type of damage to another vehicle (no matter how minute), I would never be able to forgive myself.

I also became obsessed with counting my change after a store purchase in cash, since I did not want to receive and accept a surplus, thereby "cheating" the owner. As I mentioned earlier, many of my OCD issues did center around money, and my concerns about being undercharged, not paying enough taxes, and so on. My husband would often become highly annoyed with me when it came to financial issues; if there was any discrepancy or uncertainty in a monetary transaction, I would always attempt to pay the difference and benefit the "other" party. I would explain my behavior and say to him, "If it makes me feel better, why should I not pay the difference?" Again, it made me feel better because I wanted to avoid ensuing guilt if either I or an outside party profited when we were not supposed to." The following story illustrates this:

> Once I went into a store, selected a few articles of clothing on my own, and went to the cashier to pay. She asked me, "Who helped you select these clothes?" Because I wanted her to get a commission, I said, "You did." The words just popped out of my mouth. She smiled and rang up the purchase. However, when I left the store, I felt intensely guilty because I had "lied."

If you have OCD, you probably have suffered from guilt, as I have. How does one deal with it? One way is to distinguish between false and true guilt. Before I came to terms with OCD, I never heard the term, "false guilt." After all, you "feel" just as guilty whether it is justified or not.

When my ability to distinguish between the two became more solidified, I now had another valuable tool to help me recover. Learning to evaluate and analyze the situation to determine what I should feel guilty about is a process that I absolutely had to go through. I needed to ask myself some of the following questions that pertained to the aforementioned incident:

- **What were the consequences of my actions?** Perhaps the sales person could have gotten a commission to which she was technically not entitled.

- **Did any real harm or injury result?** If she did get the commission at all, it would have been a small amount of money. If her commission was 10%, she may have gotten $6.80, since the total bill was about $68. She probably needed the money more than the store. No real harm resulted. Secondly, she also may have not even gotten the commission. I had no idea whether or not she credited herself with the sale.

- **Did I intend to do any harm or injury to someone?** Absolutely not! My intent was to let her get the commission because I wanted to be kind to a person with a low paying job. This is probably the most important question that a person can ask herself! I can honestly say that I had no intentions of harming or cheating anyone in any sort of monetary transaction.

I realize now that by asking myself these questions, my guilt was exaggerated and out of proportion for my actions, which were rather inconsequential. I made minor technicalities into catastrophic events. I was just not aware that it was my thought processes that were making me sick. I learned that OCD is a disease of false fear and false guilt. And once I realized that fact, my anxieties diminished, and I began to recover.

You can help yourself by also asking these questions when you have a guilt attack:

- What is it that I actually did?
- Would other people feel guilty if they had done the same thing?
- How would an imaginary panel of experts judge me?
- What if someone had done this to me – Would I be able to forgive him?"
- Did I intend to do harm or injury?

By answering those questions, you will be able to gain some insight as to whether or not your guilt is at all justified. The ultimate way to address guilt is to look at yourself through God's loving and forgiving eyes.

Your intentions for any action are highly significant. Did you intend to hurt anyone? God is aware of your heart and soul. If you did not have any evil intent, then you simply made a mistake, and there is no need to feel guilty. To wit, pencils have erasers because we all make mistakes at one time or another. If we did not err, then how could we learn anything? God does NOT want you to feel guilty about a minor mistake.

Suppose we are negligent, and the mistake is NOT minor. What happens in this case? God's love for us is so enormous that when we truly repent, he absolves us. If we are not aware of the mistake and don't repent, He forgives us anyway. He pardons not only our past and present sins but the sins we haven't even committed yet (Stanley, 61). Guilt is counterproductive because it diminishes our ability to serve Him. It is not God's will that we feel guilty; we choose it for ourselves. We have the alternative of choosing God's forgiveness, which is being offered to us the very moment we do make a mistake.

I no longer feel that if something "were to happen," I could not live with the guilt. What has helped is thinking that whenever I do make a mistake, God's love is so intense that He forgives me for all of my transgressions, no matter what they are. If God pardons me for my sins, then how could I defy God and NOT forgive myself? God's forgiveness is available and it is up to me to accept it.

If we accept God's forgiveness for ourselves, then we also must learn to forgive others. We are to reflect the divine Spirit that is already within us. Understandably, this can be very difficult when a person has hurt you emotionally, physically, or financially. Yet, when you allow yourself to forgive, you are ultimately benefitting yourself. Dr. Edward Hallowell, psychiatrist and author of *Dare to Forgive*, cites some possible physical health benefits of forgiving, such as lowered blood pressure and resting heart rate, decreased susceptibility to heart attack and stroke, and a strengthened immune system. The real plus of being forgiving, however, is increased happiness and clarity of thinking (7). Forgiveness is not only free, in that it costs nothing, but it frees us from the enslavement of anger and resentment (25).

I remember when my daughter, a teenager at the time, went out with her friends one night and was going to stay out later than usual. The arrangement was that she was to take a cab home, split the bill with her companions, and wake me up upon her arrival so that I would know she reached home safely. Well, she did wake me up by calling at 3:15 AM to tell me that she did not have her house key with her and demanded that I put a spare key in the mailbox. I complied, but after walking downstairs, finding a key, opening the door, and putting it in the mailbox, I was pretty much wide awake. To make matters more complicated, she did not come home until after 4 AM, which was considerably later than our arrangement.

    Finally, I went back to sleep, only to be awakened again by her, when she turned lights on and began to noisily rummage through my bedroom closet, to look for a blanket and pillow for her friend who was staying over (this was not part of our arrangement either). Negative and angry thoughts were racing through my head, thinking, "how can I go back to sleep?" If I remained angry, sleep would not have been forthcoming. Once I decided to **forgive** my daughter's thoughtlessness, however, I was able to fall asleep again. When we fret and fume, we hurt ourselves. Once we switch gears, and practice forgiveness, peace and relaxation occur automatically.

    It is also true that anger begets anger. The next morning, I started to chastise my daughter for being so inconsiderate. She yelled back at me, "If you can't sleep, take sleeping pills." Later, when I calmly explained that several interruptions during the night rendered me unable to readily fall back asleep, she said that she would remember to take her key next time. She had a loving response instead of an indignant one, once I changed my angry approach.

Dealing with the Guilt Accompanying OCD

I have suffered a great deal of guilt over relatively inconsequential and trivial matters. Yet, when I was younger, I wanted to assert myself, be independent and not conform to spiritual expectations. I exhibited general defiance toward family elders, especially my uncle and my mother. As a teenager, I remember arguing with my poor mom on pretty much a daily basis. She habitually told me what to do, such as, "Please don't leave the lights on when you leave a room – it is a waste of electricity and money. Please eat the grapes before you eat other fruit – they will go bad, and I don't want to throw out good food. Don't leave your dirty dishes in the sink", and so on. Being a stressed single parent and living on minimum wage necessitated that she be extremely frugal to make ends meet. But when it came to her wishes, I was young, unsympathetic, and non-compliant. There were many nasty, shouting matches between us. Looking back, I gave her a lot of grief about **nonsense**. My harsh words, and lack of respect and understanding for her difficult circumstances should have given me pause – I should have felt **true guilt** for my lack of empathy and cooperation.

My lack of understanding and consideration also affected my relationship with my uncle. At one point, I chose not to have contact with him for several years (as a very young adult) because I was obnoxious, hard-headed, and did not want to listen to what in hindsight, was pretty good advice. There were those ironic times where I made the very people that loved and cared for me, miserable. Yet, after several years of estrangement, I decided to resume the relationship with my uncle by surprising him on a beach board walk one day, knowing he would frequently walk a particular path. When he spotted me, he welcomed me with open, loving arms and hugs. After that moment, I decided to visit with him on a weekly basis. We resumed our relationship, which improved steadily over time. This memory provided a true insight into the **forgiving** nature of my uncle, and later on, set the foundation for my acceptance of God's forgiveness and my ultimate spirituality. When ill, I remember asking my uncle fairly frequently, "Was I good enough to you?" Despite the fact that I had caused him grief, his response was always a resounding yes. One time, he said, "If I had a magic wand, and I could change you – I would choose to change – nothing!" Those healing words stuck with me and I slowly started to absorb how profound forgiveness could be, and the true meaning of the word "grace."

I have made many mistakes in my life, especially in social situations, by acting inappropriately, being oblivious to the emotions of others and considering only one set of feelings – my own. For many years, I rebelled against God's Laws, by being self-centered, inconsiderate, envious and proud. Regardless of what I have done, (or not done)

God, in His infinite mercy has forgiven me through His unmerited love. And just as I have accepted God's forgiveness, I have learned to extend forgiveness to others.

7

Exaggerated Responsibility

People with OCD often suffer because they have an exaggerated sense of responsibility, which means that they think they are responsible for things that they are actually NOT. We envision potential harm occurring to others or ourselves, and if we don't try to prevent it, we experience guilt. We are morally decent people, but we often don't know when our responsibility to prevent harm ends.

In my OCD days, I was not able to distinguish what I was, and **was not** actually responsible for. In the height of an OCD episode, I felt guilty because I told a disadvantaged student of mine who was having trouble at home to try to study in his local library. I imagined that if he were to get robbed and beat up on the way to the library it would be my fault. The thought of harm coming to the student inhabited my mind for several days, and the guilt attack was intense, making me feel miserable and worthless.

I was able to discuss my fear with my uncle, who pointed out that the student would have to do many routine things in his neighborhood, such as attend school, go to the store, to a friend's house and so on. I did not have any control over his environment. It was his parents' responsibility to help him cope with his surroundings, not mine. In addition, the probability of the student becoming harmed from walking in his neighborhood was fairly remote. He told me to ask myself, "How many people would condemn a teacher for telling a student to 'go to the library'? That is standard educational practice." I eventually realized that I being unduly harsh on myself, by practicing self-condemnation once again.

Grayson points out in his book, *Freedom from Obsessive-Compulsive Disorder: A Personalized Recovery Program for Living with Uncertainty* that, "OCD sufferers must learn to live with the sins of irresponsibility that all of us are guilty of" (100). He talks about the survey method as a tool for OCD sufferers to recognize when their thinking is out of line. Grayson advocates comparing your thinking and behavior with that of others. If the majority of people do not feel guilty when engaging in a particular behavior, you need not feel guilty either (109). When I read about this, it had a huge impact on me. My husband had also told me that I should just observe other people, and then try to do likewise. I ignored his advice, until the same guidance came from a "professional." After becoming more enlightened, I started to make a point to observe others. If the majority of the population did not manifest a particular behavior, I made up my mind to try my very best NOT to do it either. For example, I used to cut branches from shrubs into very small pieces so they would not stick out of the garbage can. I was afraid that if a piece stuck out, and someone walked by or rode her bike near it, that person could accidentally poke out her eye. I spent a lot of time, trying to arrange my rubbish so no one could get "hurt." I had trouble throwing plastic bags away because they could theoretically fly out of the container and suffocate a lone child. Throwing out broken glass was also difficult because, in my mind, the trash collector could get cut. (I only later noticed that many sanitation workers wear gloves when they work.) I was obsessed with someone becoming injured from my garbage. However, my neighbors did not check their garbage and spend a lot of time rearranging it. They threw out gardening waste in containers where the branches stuck out over the top. They had no qualms throwing out plastic bags or broken glass. After all, it was garbage. Were people in general practicing my rituals? If the answer was "no," then I had to make a concerted effort not to do it either. I eventually stopped checking and re-arranging my garbage, and now throw out plastic bags and broken glass if I need to. I can tell you that this method worked well for me as a tool for OCD recovery. (I also realized that my husband was a pretty smart person, who was trying as best as he could to help me.)

At the height of my OCD illness, I used to exit my school and pull the door closed behind me quite a few times – I did not even consider the fact that it was self-locking. I was anxious and felt that if someone were to break into the school, steal equipment and vandalize, it would be my fault for not being diligent enough. To recover, I had to force myself NOT to check the door after I walked out of a building and acknowledge that my thinking was just the product of another OCD thought. In order to reduce the anxiety, I had to talk to myself in the following way:

> "Most people would not check the door upon leaving the building. It would be the job of the maintenance people to make sure that the self-locking doors operated properly."

My doctor pointed out that if someone did sneak in and "steal" something valuable, who would the police arrest - me or the person stealing? If the door did not self-lock, and I failed to notice, it would not have been my responsibility anyway. In addition, at that moment in time, there would also have been no consequences for my lack of action.

Dear reader, walking away is difficult. It is extremely tempting to check the door "just one more time" in order to reduce that horrible anxiety. It is not easy to "just leave" when you are in the midst of an OCD attack.

Exaggerated Responsibility

However, consider the alternative. If you give in to the checking you will reduce your anxiety for a short time. But as was mentioned earlier, our checking is like an addictive drug – the more you check, the more you will need to check again, and again. And we know the long-term consequences of checking – wasted time, effort and more misery. The irony is, that after all the checking, you will eventually have anxiety anyway. Can you put up with the short-term torture for long term gain? Can you say to yourself, "The anxiety will dissipate over time?" When you decide to talk to yourself compassionately, and not check repetitively, you will achieve great gains in your own healing. Can you mentally put yourself in the future, and think how nice it would be **not** to feel this compulsion?

    I also remember feeling compelled to pick up pieces of glass on the sidewalk, so that a child or a barefoot individual would not get "hurt." First of all, I could never do it perfectly enough. I always had doubt about whether I missed a small fragment. Secondly, in order to overcome the anxiety (and the compulsion) I had to say to myself:

> "Did I put the glass there? If I did not put the glass there, I should not condemn myself for not picking it up. Did I see other people picking up glass? After actually watching people as they walked obliviously right by the glass, the answer was a resounding 'no.'

Isn't foot injury a risk that an individual assumes when she chooses to walk barefoot? Aren't people responsible for their own actions? Isn't it a parent's responsibility to see that her child will not pick up glass? Finally, in the absolute worst case, if someone were to actually step on a small piece of glass, what damage could potentially occur? I suppose it would be temporarily a little painful and he would bleed somewhat."

I should point out that I might every so often pick up a glass bottle from a street curb, so that a car won't crush it and glass fragments won't be distributed. I don't want someone (including myself) getting a flat tire when they park their car. The key here is that I no longer feel compelled to do it. When I do pick up glass ever so rarely, I congratulate myself for trying to be a civic-minded person, rather than condemning myself and feeling guilty if I don't do it. I also know that I am a morally decent person even if I don't go around combing the streets for glass.

I frequently had trouble establishing where my line of responsibility ended, which is typical of many OCD sufferers. Jeff Bell, author of *Rewind, Replay, and Repeat: A Memoir of Obsessive – Compulsive Disorder*, describes his ordeal battling OCD while simultaneously supporting his family as a co-anchor newsman on a radio station in San Francisco.

Exaggerated Responsibility

In his memoir, he humorously calls himself "Captain Hazard" because of his attempts to prevent "harm." For example, Bell accidentally dropped a piece of Reese's Peanut Butter Cup on a sidewalk in downtown San Francisco and spent five minutes combing a street corner in order to pick it up so that no harm would come to anyone (123-124). He also describes an incident whereby his dripping umbrella creates a couple of small droplets on the floor of a supermarket and Bell is worried that his actions may cause others to slip. He informs the store, who has an employee come and mop it up. The irony is that the assigned cleanup person says that he cannot even find the puddle (123). This might sound laughable to the average mentally healthy person. However, I can tell you my fear and behavior were very similar to that of Jeff Bell. We see exaggerated, negative consequences resulting from our actions. We respond to the voices of OCD - false fear, false guilt, and hyper-responsibility which compels us to behave in a ludicrous fashion until we learn how to think and behave otherwise.

As OCD sufferers, we can apply Reinhold Niebuhr's Serenity Prayer (1934):

> "God grant me the ability to accept what I cannot change, the courage to change the things I can, and the wisdom to know the difference."

We have to realize where our boundaries of accountability end, since we cannot hold ourselves responsible for the actions of others. Much of what occurs in our environment is out of our control. We CANNOT save the entire world. If we actually overcome our OCD, then we are in so much better condition to benefit our fellow human beings and positively impact society, instead of merely attempting to temporarily reduce our anxiety and false sense of guilt. We try to do our best and let God do the rest.

8

The Same Mind that Can Make You Sick Can Make You Well

The mind is extremely powerful. When scientists wish to study the effects of drugs or medication, control and experimental groups are established. The experimental group receives the actual drug being investigated, while the control group receives a placebo. The placebo may be a harmless sugar pill, a salt-water solution, or tablet that imitates the actual drug, so that participants will not know the difference between the drug being studied and the inert substance, and consequently will not know to which group they are assigned. Ironically enough, when placebos are given to patients, they improve, which is known as the "placebo effect." At one time, the beneficial effects were assumed to be psychological; a person benefited by taking a pill merely because he expected the pill or the injection to work. However, scientists are now finding that a placebo not only affects someone psychologically, but physiologically as well. When a patient expects to heal, the brain produces its own natural painkillers, called endogenous opioids. New research shows there is an actual pain-processing network that can "inhibit pain processing in the spinal cord, thereby minimizing pain responses in the brain" (O'Callaghan). This has profound implications: **thinking that you will heal actually causes you to heal.**

People who have complained about the inability to sleep at times have been given pills that they think are sleeping aids, when in fact they are innocuous. The power of belief, however, is so strong that they go to sleep. The pills are placebos, but because the person believes the pill will be effective, it becomes effective. The same is true for pain medication. When soldiers had pain as a result of injury, they sometimes were given an injection of saline solution instead of pain relieving medicine on the battlefield. Yet, they actually experienced decreased pain because they believed they were getting an efficacious treatment. Very often, what you believe becomes a self-fulfilling prophecy.

Why do advertisers pay millions of dollars for the privilege of a 30 second spot on television? Because the power of suggestion works – advertising increases sales. Man has a vulnerability to believe without the necessity of proof or validity. Look at the case of Bernie Madoff, the infamous con man who was arrested in 2013. People were very willing to invest their money with him merely on the suggestion that they could get high but unrealistic returns. Their power of belief was so strong that some individuals invested all of their assets only to discover that they participated in a Ponzi scheme, whereby Madoff merely returned high yields with money received from other investors. Some of Madoff's victims became destitute in the end. Apparently, Madoff's ability to influence people and cater to their own greed was so mesmerizing that they were willing to part with their life long savings. **What you believe has dramatic consequences.**

What is Anxiety and Why Does It Occur?

OCD is characterized as an anxiety disorder. We know that anxiety is extremely uncomfortable, yet, in an emergency situation it is very necessary. For example, a mother might become very anxious if she sees her child run into the street with oncoming traffic. She would have a normal "flight or fight" response, equipping her body for action in extraordinary circumstances, so that she could either fight or flee a threatening situation. God gave us the ability to feel anxious as a self-preservation mechanism, in which an abundance of certain catecholamine hormones, adrenaline and noradrenalin, are released to prepare the entire body for action. This physiological response can include increased heart and breathing rate, dilation of blood to the muscles, constriction of blood vessels to other body parts, shaking, a slowing of digestion, a release of fat and glucose, acceleration of reflexes, and pupil dilation. Diversion of the blood from the stomach to the muscles and an increase in nutrients to those bodily areas that support escape or aggression, can be very useful in potentially life-threatening circumstances.

However, humans can exhibit this same response when it is completely **unnecessary**. It is not unusual for people with OCD to suffer from prolonged anxiety when there is no threatening situation. Lucinda Bassett summarized the symptoms of anxiety in her book, *From Panic to Power* (37):

- Sleepless nights, marked by tossing and turning, and more worry about not being able to sleep.
- Inability to concentrate on a specific task, or unable to do a job.
- A reduction in appetite, or indigestion.
- A feeling of being overwhelmed by life in general.
- A feeling of "nervousness," trembling, or shaking.
- Racing heart rate.

The next level of anxiety is a panic attack, a fearful reaction so severe that physical symptoms, such as shortness of breath, chest pains, dizziness, heart palpitations, and extreme jitteriness can be experienced. Anxiety can leave you feeling depressed, fatigued, and hopeless (Bassett, 25). I have had chronic anxiety and panic attacks at times, and I can tell you that they are quite psychologically devastating. Living with obsessive worry is really not "living" at all.

What is the Difference between Concern and Anxiety?

In a nutshell, concern is beneficial, while anxiety is not. A certain amount of concern is healthy and normal. It is perfectly acceptable to be concerned about the health of your family, doing a good job, having enough resources to meet your needs, and so on. Concern prompts us to positive action. If we care about our health, we will try to eat a well-balanced diet and exercise. If we care about our children, we will take an active interest in what they are doing, their academic performance, and who they associate with. We will try to give them the best guidance we can, and be there for them when times are tough. A person may be "concerned" about paying his bills. That person will then hopefully try to reduce his expenses, downsize, take a second job, or alter his lifestyle. However, if that same person sees a bleak future, emotionally falls apart, and is paralyzed with inaction, that is characteristic of anxiety. Sleepless nights, irritability, and imagining the worst-case scenario all lead to counterproductive anxiety, rob us of our peace and are NOT God's will for us (Stanley, 122-3).

What Causes Anxiety?

There is one simple answer – "anxiety is caused by

the way we think" (Bassett, 89). Our thoughts shape the way we speak to ourselves and have potent consequences. I can attest to the fact that my thoughts have made me sick enough to be hospitalized. Our self-talk can be very constructive and enable us to do great things, or it can ruin us. Suppose, for example, a person gets a poor review from his employer. His inner dialogue can sound something like this:

> "I know that my work is below par and that my boss dislikes me. I probably will get fired in the near future. How will I support myself and pay my bills? Life is unfair and totally against me."

Such negative inner dialogue can be detrimental. The person becomes overwhelmed and has made a minor incident into a catastrophe, which has not even happened. Such thinking can cause emotional turmoil, and distress. Yet it need not be that way.

Given the exact same conditions, however, a person's inner dialogue can be quite different and look like this:

> "I will try to be more reflective of my work and see if my supervisor actually has a valid point. Let me see if I can work on my weaknesses and improve. If

The Same Mind That Can Make You Sick Can Make You Well

> I try my best, we should see some improvement and I will hopefully get a better review next time."

In this case, the mindset is much more positive, and leads to problem solving and learning. It is obvious which type of thinking benefits the individual and others around him. OCD thoughts are often negative, worst case scenario thoughts, twisted in such a way to cause anguish, guilt and anxiety.

The good news, though, is that the same mind that can make us sick can also make us well. I began to get well after I accepted the following truism: we all have choices in how we think and react. It requires practice, but we can choose, and change our thought patterns (Bassett, 32).

The idea that our thoughts determine our emotions and our behavioral responses is not new. In *Proverbs 23:7,* the *Bible* states, "as he thinketh in his heart, so is he." Epictetus (55 AD – 135AD), a Roman (Greek born) philosopher and speaker noted:

- "It's not what happens to you, but how you react to it that matters."
- "Men are disturbed, not by things, but by the view they take of them."

Once we accept the premise that we are responsible for our

thoughts, and that we can change them with God's help, we are well on our way to controlling our emotions and reducing our anxiety that feeds the OCD.

My Darkest Thoughts – When My Mind Made Me Sick

As I mentioned before, I was hospitalized because my tormenting thoughts made me feel suicidal. I would have visions of death, and trouble concentrating on my external surroundings. Basically, I tried to seclude myself so I would not have to converse with anyone. One of my major anxieties was a fear that my family was going to "hell" because they expressed doubts about a biblical text that "Jesus Christ is the son of God." (I was in contact with very fundamentalist Christians that swore this was the case.) I felt hopeless, never laughed or smiled during this time, and had no appetite. The simple pleasures of life, such as playing tennis, walking on the beach, and enjoying a friendship had evaporated. My mind was held captive to negative and constantly reoccurring destructive thoughts. I was so torn about the afterlife of my family that death became appealing as a respite from my misery. As I mentioned before in Chapter 3, I was able to reconcile this issue, and no longer dwell on the afterlife – my personal view is that I don't know what happens after we die.

I had a cousin, who lived in another country, but

whom I had met several times, and knew her and her family fairly well. At the age of 62, she committed suicide, on her third attempt. I was terrified of repeating her history – leaving my children a note and ending my life. Fears from the reactions of others – my children, husband, friends, neighbors and colleagues – ruminated in my mind.

Obsessions of contracting Lyme disease, and/or developing osteoporosis, any number of cancers (and their resulting complications), fears of my uncle dying (and having no one to help me,) losing my mind, not sleeping, and harming others through my own negligence, all held my mind captive at one time or another, contributing to my depression and despair. When I once discussed my fears with a psychiatrist, he simply stated, "If you are not afraid of the ocean, you will be afraid of the police. If it is not the police, it will be sky, etc." Succinctly put, I was afraid of everything. At one point, my uncle pointed out that I feared fear itself. Yet my he calmly encouraged me to battle every phobia, albeit one at a time, by giving me a toolbox of coping skills to aid in my recovery.

Substituting a Positive Thought for a Negative Thought

I read the story of author and speaker Lucinda Bassett's life and found that she recovered from a life of anxiety and panic attacks to become the Director of the

Midwest Anxiety Disorders Treatment Center. She now helps anxious people overcome their habit of negative thinking (150). She suggests carrying around a notebook and writing down negative thoughts, so that we become aware of them. This makes it easier to become pro-active and change them to positive thoughts. Although this requires a great deal of time and commitment, the results speak for themselves. Bassett observed that people who had previously suffered from anxiety were at first writing pages and pages of notes filled with negative thoughts. Over weeks of practice using positive thought substitution, however, their negative thinking diminished both on the written page, and more importantly, in the mind. The consequence of the exercise was diminishing anxiety (151).

    I can personally attest that this has been true for me. Once my thinking changed, my anxiety vaporized. I have far less sleeping difficulty, no more panic attacks, nor loss of appetite, and am now a normal weight as opposed to being very thin during the height of my illness.

    We have the option – instead of entertaining thoughts of calamity, we can entertain thoughts of peace and goodness. Negative thoughts are like weeds. Once they establish themselves in the ground, they become more difficult to pull out. When the first twinge of a negative thought penetrates our consciousness, we must try to substitute it with a more wholesome, positive thought, so it will not take root. We must try to substitute the "weed" thoughts with those of God's forgiveness and peace and consider the beauty of those thoughts.

Here are some examples of negative OCD thoughts, and positive ones to counteract them.

Negative	Positive
I have hit rock bottom.	There is no way to go but upward. I have to be patient, but I will recover from OCD, one day at a time.
It is not fair that I have OCD, and that I am suffering.	God will not give me more than I can bear. God will help me heal. Let me thank Him that the illness is treatable.
I will never recover from OCD.	Millions of people have recovered from this illness. With God's help, there is no reason why I can't recover too.
I am so afraid of hurting someone.	God knows my heart, and He knows that I have never intended to hurt anyone. That is what really counts.
I am afraid of making a mistake.	I should strive for God's standards, not human ones. God's forgiveness is predicated on us making mistakes.
It is so difficult to battle	Once I recognize my true

OCD.	identity as a child of God, my battle will seem easy.
I don't have a good support system right now.	God is my ever-present support system. Once I have a real relationship with God, I have the support I need.

A grandfather was telling his granddaughter that inside of everyone are two lions having a tremendous battle. One lion represents the emotions of fear and guilt, while the other represents the emotions of peace and love. The little girl responded, "Which one wins?" The grandfather replied, "It depends on the one you feed."

Which emotion are you feeding? Remember, you are accountable for what you entertain in your mind. What you feed will either give you serenity or anxiety. If your mission is peace, then you need to fill your mind with peaceful thoughts. And that becomes much easier when you think about God. I have had obsessive thoughts and it is true that they are difficult to eradicate. However, you can certainly challenge and talk back to them. (For more detail, see Chapter 9.) After you diminish their importance and speak back to them, they occur less frequently and intensely. My obsessive thoughts have, to a great extent, disappeared!

There are many scriptural paradigms on how to think and what to think about. Here are some words of wisdom from the *New Testament of the Bible*, and this is one of my favorites:

> *Phil. 4:8*: "Finally brothers, whatever is true, whatever is noble, whatever is right, whatever is pure, whatever is lovely, whatever is admirable – if anything is excellent or praiseworthy – think about such things."

We benefit by thinking about what is good in the world. Here is a partial and brief list of what I like to think about in order to enhance my spirituality and peace:

- The beauty of nature, which is God's creation
- God's unconditional love
- How I can support my family
- God's continuing forgiveness
- The diversity of life
- Finding the Divine in every human being
- Joyous moments in my life
- Expressing positive goals, I am setting for myself
- How to express love and kindness to specific people
- All the blessings that God has bestowed upon me
- What I can do to make the world a better place
- How I can be a better servant to God and

humanity
- How I can improve upon a given situation
- How I can help those less fortunate than myself

We can only entertain one thought at a time and cannot practice negative thinking if we are thinking about goodness. We also have the ability to choose thoughts that are most beneficial to us. We can think that God loves unconditionally, and that peace is always there for us, instead of having worrisome thoughts about nonsense in many cases.

Don't Personalize Other People's Troubles and Make Them Your Own

People that are anxious tend to hear other people's troubles, and then identify with them (Bassett, 80). My 91-year-old relative said she couldn't sleep if she had a doctor's appointment the next day. After hearing the statement, I started to personalize it and say to myself, "what if that happened to me?" I became so worried about not sleeping, that of course, I did not sleep. What an unproductive thought! There was absolutely no reason in the world why I should not have slept. Instead, I should have said to myself, "I feel sorry for that lady. Thank God I do not have that problem." Once I started feeling true compassion for the person (you can't feign this) instead of identifying with her problem, I felt much less anxious and was better able to relate to her.

Write down all the things in your life that you can be grateful for, such as a roof over your head, a warm home in the winter, the people that care about you, a loving pet, your ability to walk and to enjoy your food, and countless other blessings given to us. God has given us roses to smell, beautiful birds to listen to, and beaches to admire. Everything here on this earth belongs to the God who has already provided for us. Our divine plan is not to be fearful. Take the time to "smell the roses" and develop an attitude of gratitude for His gifts.

In addition, you can use powers of positive thinking, not only for yourself, but also for the benefit of the people with whom you come into contact. When a person approaches you with a problem, develop a philosophy and try to use your mental energies to problem solve, in order to achieve a positive outcome, rather than just lending an ear. By attempting to problem-solve, you end up benefiting yourself as much as the person you are helping.

The "What if" Syndrome

Anxious people have a tendency to overreact, and to magnify risk to a very high level, succumbing to the "what if" syndrome (Bassett, 91). I used to be one big over-reactor. I imagined one negative scenario after another, usually beginning with the words "what if" or "suppose."

I remember feeling guilty about having students include their names on their video projects. They were asked to create scripts, and then act them out in a one-minute video detailing a historical event by acting as newscasters. I felt that it would be more motivating to have them research a topic, write a short script, act it out, and edit the video, as opposed to reading some material and writing a report. When they announced each other, they said their names in the video. I felt incredibly guilty. My reasoning was as follows: What if someone could possibly upload the videos onto the Internet? A child molester could see the videos of the children. What if this molester came to the school and got into the schoolyard? What if he then recognized one of the children in the video and approached him or her? What if a student walked away with the molester and he violated them?

What was exactly my role in the situation? I had allowed students to say their names in the video. When I told my doctor about this fear, which I had agonized over, he actually laughed, and said, "You did not put the videos on the Internet. Videos cannot be uploaded without parental consent, which you did not even ask for. Furthermore, the chance of a supposed molester being able to identify a school in a video and approach the kid in a schoolyard is infinitesimal. It is also a parent's responsibility to pick up his child from school. What are you picturing – that a molester will say to a child, 'Come with me,' and the child will voluntarily go because a stranger knows his name? You are worried about NONSENSE." I was then instructed NOT to remove the student names from the video since a student can be very proud of his name and his work. It was a creative project, and I was to congratulate myself on doing such an interesting, innovative project with my children.

The following story is another good example of how we make ourselves anxious and miserable over nothing, by entertaining spiraling negative thoughts. I have a friend who became very alarmed one Saturday when she noticed that her stool was red after going to the bathroom. She called a gastroenterologist and he told her she needed an MRI right away. We thought that this was a possible sign of colon cancer. My friend became quite anxious and did not sleep well for a few nights, worrying and thinking, "What if I need surgery, chemotherapy, and radiation?" Scenarios of "what ifs" crept into her mind.

After a week, I called and asked my friend if the doctor had found out the cause of her red stool. He did. She had eaten cooked beets the past Saturday, which gave her a "red" stool that she assumed to be blood. In the end, it was a relief, and somewhat funny. But just imagine – she went through all that unnecessary agony for nothing. I, too, have worried endlessly over figments of my own imagination. Our minds can cause physical and mental havoc when we jump to false conclusions.

My uncle gave me a ludicrous analogy of "what if" scenarios.

> "I stubbed my toe. It is throbbing. What if it hurts so much that I can't walk? If I can't walk, then I will watch TV all day and eat junk food. What if I eat so much junk food that I become severely overweight? What if I become so overweight that I get a heart attack? What if I die?"

We can make ourselves crazy with a spiraling negative thought process that begins with a trivial incident, like stubbing a toe. We can also choose to NOT do this.

You might have a "what if" scenario that is serious. I had such a case. When I was ill, I thought, "What if I get so sick that I can NOT work and lose my job?" My scenario materialized. I lost my job, the ability to pay bills, and my self-esteem (temporarily, until I discovered my true identity as a child of God). Once I was not working, of course, I could not contribute to the family financially. Right then and there my life changed because of my negative "what if" thinking.

My Uncle Joey had a saying, "Just as there is a law of conservation of matter and energy (it cannot be created or destroyed, but changed from one form to another), **there is a law of equivalency in life; what you lose in one area you gain in another**." Okay, I lost my financial independence for the time being. I had time on my hands. So instead of pursuing money, I pursued recovery, which led to pursuing spirituality and examining what is important in life, such as a sense of purpose.

Stop the "What if" Scenarios All Together.

Notice that my OCD thoughts are always negative. Anxiety sufferers mentally ask themselves: what if "such and such" happened, and each speculation is one horrible worst-case scenario after another. We can help ourselves enormously if we stop imagining the catastrophes as a done deal. It helps getting rid of the words "what if", or "suppose" followed by a series of negative outcomes. The minute your mind starts with a "what if," substitute another thought. Say to yourself, **"Whatever happens, happens. God is in charge, not me."**

Change the Negative Scenario into a Positive One (Bassett, 101)

Now I am trying to use my same creative imagination

to be helpful and dream about positive possibilities. Here are some of my new thoughts: What if I:

- Exercised the love that is in me to my family members and to my neighbors?
- Focused on my gratitude I feel for my husband who loves me in sickness and in health, and for my two daughters?
- Applied spiritual principles on a constant basis in guiding my life?
- No longer feared failure?
- Did not make up imaginary catastrophes anymore?
- Realized God's GOOD plan for my life?
- Tried to help others overcome their OCD?
- Used my own experience to touch the lives of others in a wonderful way?

The new scenarios produce inspiration, serenity, and problem solving. Don't deny God the opportunity to work in you and through you to lead a more fulfilling and peaceful life. God is there, waiting to help you contemplate and implement a good plan.

You can make the positive scenarios humorous, if you want to (Bassett 78)

Let's turn the tables inside our heads, for a change, and

imagine the following positive scenario:

- What if I walked along the street and picked up a plastic bag?
- What if the bag contained $100 million dollars?
- What if the bag was completely unidentified and there was no way to trace the owner?
- What if I had to keep all the money myself? What would I do?

I suppose this case is theoretically possible, but guess what? It is never going to happen. Most likely, the mental garbage we have been dreaming up has never materialized and never will. The above situation is merely one example of how we can fabricate unnecessary scenarios that are highly improbable.

See a Situation from a Different (more positive) Perspective

You can analyze a situation from many different angles. I used to have contamination fears. One time, when many students at our local elementary school were getting sick, I became fearful of my own daughters "catching" germs from other children. My children did in fact get sick a great deal in the lower grades; over the course of a year in elementary school either one or the other had strep throat about once a month. Instead of getting upset about germs and sickness, I considered the same situation from a constructive perspective, and my fears dissipated. I said to myself, "Germs are everywhere. When kids come into contact with germs and become ill, they are exercising their immune systems. Exposure is necessary for them to build up their antibodies, so that they do not subsequently become sick." Here was an alternate, more positive way to look at this particular situation.

Change your Thoughts and You Change Your Brain Chemistry

Dr. Jeffrey M. Schwartz, a psychiatrist and researcher at the UCLA School of Medicine, and author of *Brain Lock: Free Yourself from Obsessive Compulsive Behavior*, developed a four-step help method to help his OCD patients effectively manage the illness. In essence, patients are asked to comply with the following four steps, or the four "Rs":

> **Relabel**: recognize that the intrusive thoughts and urges are the result of OCD thinking.
> **Reattribute**: understand that the thought or urge is due to a malfunction in brain circuitry.
> **Refocus**: while the OCD thought or urge is occurring, deliberately switch to another, preferably

enjoyable, behavior for at least several minutes or longer, at which time the anxiety should eventually decrease.

Revalue: Reevaluate the condition after refocusing, and understand that the OCD thought is not significant; it is a thought, not an event.

I have used this technique now and then when I have intrusive thoughts. I make chili for a church that hosts a dinner for anyone in need every Sunday and am happy to contribute to this charitable effort. One day I used the tip of a sharp knife while trying to cut frozen turkey meat into smaller pieces to defrost them more quickly. I used enough force to break the knife tip, and there was a piece of metal in the frozen meat. Not wanting to use the meat, and "be safe," I discarded it, because I did not want to harm anyone, which I suppose, was normal. I subsequently used the same knife (with the tip removed) to cut more frozen meat for another batch of chili. Intrusive thoughts came into my mind – that the tip of the knife could have been broken again, and perhaps there were remnants of the knife in the meat that I did not perceive, which could potentially injure a person eating the chili. This time, however, I said to myself, "I did not see evidence for this scenario. In fact, I used the blade, not the knife tip to cut. This is an OCD thought. I get these thoughts because I have a residual brain disorder. It is OCD – it is not me." I was able to let go of this horrible thought and think of something more pleasant, with the understanding that I will get OCD thoughts once in a while, but I can manage them. I used the meat, cooked my chili, and donated to our Sunday dinner program. Through some training, I learned to distinguish between something that could have been a real threat and just another OCD falsehood.

What is absolutely astounding about Schwartz's research is that when patients learned how to apply the "4 R" technique after ten weeks of practice and actually changed their thinking, their brain chemistry changed as well. Before treatment, OCD patients were given positron emission tomography scans of their brains, and certain areas of their brain appeared very active. After the treatment, PET scans were again taken of the individuals that were successful in managing their OCD, and the activity in these same areas was significantly reduced. There was a strong correlation between the metabolic changes in the brain and the severity ratings of OCD symptoms (58). It should also be noted that none of the patients in this particular study was on any medication, so Schwartz concluded that it was the change in thought patterns that caused the change in the brain chemistry. The essential takeaway of this study was that cognitive behavioral therapy, the goal of which is to change thought process, actually changes brain function (60). Just think about this: **you can influence your own brain chemistry by changing your thoughts**. That is one of the most empowering statements I have ever heard and lends credence to the idea that the mind is incredibly influential.

You are what you think you are. You are your thoughts. **The same mind that can make you sick can make you well. Change your thinking and you will heal yourself.** Pray to God and He will help you with this process.

9

Challenge and Analyze Your OCD

The first positive step in combating OCD thoughts is to recognize that you do have this illness. The second step would be to challenge your thoughts. I used to listen to my OCD thoughts and entertained them just as if they were real events. I did not distinguish OCD thoughts from ordinary ones, and consequently succumbed to their negative impact. After I was told my thoughts were actually causing the illness, I questioned my ability to distinguish OCD from normal thoughts. After much suffering and anguish, I eventually learned that my "doubt" was just the voice of OCD once again. OCD thoughts may vary in content, but they are all cut from the same cloth, and have several identifiable characteristics affecting people that are susceptible to OCD. These thoughts:

- Produce intense guilt, making you feel awful because they cause great self-condemnation.
- Are precisely that, thoughts - NOT events. There is no supporting evidence for the beliefs that constantly repeat in our minds, creating doubt about whether we "checked" something thoroughly or if we were "perfect" enough.

- Start with a "what if" catastrophic scenario that is a stretch of the imagination, sometimes to the point of being ludicrous to an outsider.
- Are unwanted, intrusive, and recurrent (Osborn, 31-33).
- Are terrorizing, producing substantial anxiety and discomfort.

When I became more and more adept at identifying my own OCD thoughts while my mind was wandering, half of my battle against the illness was already won.

Dr. Jonathan Grayson, in his book, *Freedom from Obsessive Compulsive Disorder*, discusses several types of thinking characteristic to OCD sufferers. The umbrella term for this type of thinking he uses is "cognitive distortions." Examples include the **intolerance for uncertainty, all or none thinking, thought-action fusion, inflated responsibility, and excessive concern for thought control** (96). When we recognize these distortions in our thinking, we can more readily challenge our fallacious thoughts.

Intolerance for Uncertainty

I was classically intolerant of uncertainty. Sufferers want assurance that something is one hundred percent safe, and that our negative imagined catastrophes will absolutely

NEVER happen. Grayson points out that this intolerance is a central flaw in OCD thinking (97). Life is inherently risky, and to overcome OCD, we have to accept uncertainty.

    I was characteristically very risk adverse in many areas of my life. My husband and I were left with a small inheritance when my mom died and toyed with the idea of buying a piece of rental property. Had we done that (in hindsight), we would have been financially set in our retirement. But we did not invest, because I could not deal with even a slight risk. I was a very good student in college with a high GPA and applied to dental school and law school. I was accepted but did not enroll because it was expensive, and I did not want to take out loans; I could not tolerate the risk of debt. (There were many other reasons I did not pursue these professions, such as the inability to defend a client, who "might be guilty.") My aversion to risk was extreme when it came to safety concerns. I was: afraid to climb a small ladder (even though I was in good physical condition), afraid to use the microwave oven (because of the "radiation"), afraid of arranging a block party because if someone became injured, I could get sued, afraid of leaving appliances plugged in, because a fire could start, afraid of taking medications because of potential side effects, and afraid of many other things involved in common, ordinary life. It got to a point where I was afraid of my own shadow, missed out on a lot of opportunities and forfeited a great deal of joy – such as learning how (and gaining the confidence) to do things for myself, taking a medication that could benefit me, and arranging fun events for myself and others.

    I have now become more adept at accepting uncertainty as a normal part of life, loosening the chains of OCD. There are negative consequences to never attempting to take risks at all. I used to have a morbid fear of going on nature hikes in the Long Island area because I did not want to risk getting bit by a tick that could possibly give me Lyme disease. It was very ironic when, two of my family members, who never go hiking, were diagnosed with Lyme after showing symptoms. At any rate, my fear caused me to miss out on enjoying many things - the beauty of the fall foliage turning brilliant colors, the health benefits of walking in the outdoors, and the companionship of other nature lovers. Now, I do walk on nature trails, but dress appropriately in long sleeves and pants tucked into my boots, check my body after walking, stay on the trail, and monitor the date after my walks so that in the event I do get some symptoms, I can get medical attention right away. In other words, I take the proper precautions, rather than avoid the activity altogether. I now do more things on my own, use ladders and power tools, take medication, and try to cultivate a sense of adventure by planning new experiences. I have to endure some risk to reap the benefits of a joyous activity; living life involves a series of trade-offs.

Black and White Thinking (or All or None Thinking)

This is apparent when we believe something is hazardous or non-hazardous, good or bad, risky or safe; there is no in between. I have exhibited this type of thinking many times. Some examples are:

- If someone goes to church or place of worship, he or she is a good person.
- People that like to shop are materialistic, and therefore not spiritual.
- Underage teens that drink alcohol are bad kids.

What nonsense and misinterpretation! First of all, the fact that people attend church services does not make them good. Their actions dictate goodness, or the lack of it. I have learned the hard way that religious does not mean ethical. We were once rear-ended after my husband stopped at a red light by a religious man who owned a moving van. He had no car insurance and refused to pay our damages. We had to take him to small claims court to recover the cost of fixing our car. Knowing full well that he was guilty, he finally paid us the day before he had to appear in court. Secondly, I have gotten to know a couple of people that like to shop yet are extremely generous and care deeply about others. Finally, teens are exploratory and may experiment with alcohol, and even drugs, despite the fact that they are smart, nice kids. Because their brains are not yet mature, they may make somewhat poor choices at times. I can think of instances where my own daughters sometimes made poor choices, especially during the teen years. I did – we all did, and sometimes still do. Hopefully, we learn from our mistakes, and acquire more wisdom as we get older.

Another example of my all or none thinking was my view that stealing was "always" bad. Ask yourself, "If a poverty-stricken mother steals bread to feed her hungry children, is that bad? Or good?" Can the actions of the mother could be justified? Things are often neither bad nor good, but somewhere in between.

I remember learning about low frequency, long wavelength radiation and reading an article about the safety of microwaves. I became very averse to using a microwave oven due to my fears of microwave radiation leakage and refused to have one in my house for a long time. I wanted assurance that either this type of radiation was one hundred percent safe, or a microwave that was one hundred percent leak proof. I found out that the U.S. Department of Health has set a standard for maximum allowable microwave leakage. Unfortunately, no one really knows what a "safe" level of microwave exposure is. I reasoned that if I were concerned about radiation leakage from an appliance, then I should be concerned about background radiation from an airport, cell phone or computer. Should I eliminate cell phones and computers from my life as well? I began to see that microwave radiation was discussed in relative terms, and any radiation that fell below a certain guideline was deemed "relatively safe" for the time being. The ultimate safety of microwave radiation is very difficult to determine scientifically. It is a complex issue and is still under investigation. Risk must be seen in relative terms.

My husband eventually bought a microwave despite my protests, citing that "millions of people use it." I finally saw the convenience of the appliance, and began to use it too, enjoying the benefits of rapidly heating up food. However, when I do turn it on, I stand an arm's length (or more) away from it, because I know that the further removed from the machine I am, the more my exposure of radiation leakage is minimized. So instead of becoming impossibly rigid, I have tried to become more flexible and realize that my avoidance of any contamination or risk is impossible.

Thought-action Fusion

Basically, OCDers turn thoughts into actual events. We react to a terrible thought as if it had actually happened, even though it did not. At one point, I had a fear of "poisoning" members outside my family with germs and contamination. I had ordered pizza and soda for some teenage visitors at my home. One of them asked me for ice so that she could add it to her soda. Without hesitation, I gave her some ice from my freezer that had been in contact with a cardboard container of ice cream. Afterward, I chastised myself and felt incredibly guilty for doing so. My (false) reasoning was as follows: dirty, germ-laden hands of outsiders could have touched the cardboard box of ice cream. The ice came into contact with the container, so it became "contaminated" with germs as well. The girl put the ice into her cup of soda, drank it, and introduced the germs into her system. I knew she was prone to infections, and now I was the "responsible" person giving her contaminated ice. I felt just as guilty as if I had intentionally poisoned her, and kept dwelling on her "supposed" illness, as if it really had occurred.

    Yet, it was all conjecture that she would get sick. That was my old thinking pattern. In fact, she did not get sick. Nothing happened. I really should have said to myself, "Germs are everywhere, and are virtually impossible to avoid. In addition, many germs cannot survive in freezing temperatures, thereby reducing the probability of germ contamination."

Inflated Responsibility

We believe we are responsible for preventing any possible harm to others or ourselves. We have trouble determining where someone else's responsibility starts and where ours ends. We can make ourselves responsible for any situation that we imagine. I was so good at creating negative scenarios and being hyper responsible that I devoted Chapter 7 to this topic.

Excessive Concern about Controlling our Thoughts

We become thoroughly focused on an OCD thought and interpret it to mean that we are somehow "evil" because we have such thoughts. Doubt can set in, and then we fear we might act on the thought. We can also fear that this thought will "never" go away, when in fact it will go away over time. I personally have forgotten many of my OCD thoughts.

Ways to Challenge, Counteract, or Talk Back to our OCD Thoughts

You need not be a slave to your OCD thoughts. You can master, analyze, challenge, and talk back to them. The greatest battles will take place in your own mind, and you can be victorious. I am an ordinary person and if I succeeded, so can you. Grayson has cited several methods OCD sufferers have used to successfully combat these thoughts, such as the **survey, double standard,** and **Socratic questioning** methods (104). I have personally used all of these and have added a couple of others.

Survey Method

Take notice: do other people do what you are doing? Do they wash their hands fifty times per day? Do they check their gas stoves, electrical appliances and faucets repetitively? Observe others closely, and you will find that, no, they usually don't. And guess what – they survive and are fine. They don't do the things you do because they are NOT necessary. And if others are not doing it, you don't need to do it either.

I remember going on a birding walk in a national park. We were walking on a trail, but there were quite a few tree branches that stuck out into the path. I immediately began to worry and think, "Someone could get poked by a branch. What if he accidentally got poked in the eye? Maybe I should start clipping off the branches as I walk by to prevent possible harm." I had to talk back to this thought in the following manner:

> "Do you see other people clipping branches? If you don't see this, then you should not do it. Your goal is to be like everybody else. You cannot spare the world from potential harm every time. In addition,

if you start clipping the branches that are sticking out into the trail, they will only grow back. Is this how you want to spend your life? Or do you want to learn to overcome your OCD, function and be of real use to your family and to society? Remember, no matter what you do or don't do, God loves you."

After speaking to myself in this fashion, I did not clip branches. My anxiety eventually dissipated, and I had another victory against OCD.

The Double Standard Method

If we make a mistake and harm someone by our negligence, we feel that it would be unforgivable. If someone were to make the same mistake we fear, would we condemn the person or would we excuse him? My husband accidently once left the patio door unlocked and wide open overnight. (By the way, nothing happened.) When I got up the next morning and noticed it, I did not yell, or get upset. I pointed it out to him and left it at that. He is human and made this particular mistake once in 30 years of marriage. It was not difficult for me to overlook my husband's oversight. By the same token, I should pardon myself if I were to make the same error. You can apply the same logic. If you can absolve someone else for a mistake, why couldn't you absolve yourself? And, if you cannot forgive someone for the error, then you need to work on your spirituality. **Forgiveness benefits both the forgiven and the forgiver.**

Socratic Questioning Method

When my children were small, I was not ready to admit that I had OCD. I suffered from "irrational" fears, although they did not seem irrational at the time. I worried that my children would conceal themselves in suitcases, dishwashers, and washing machines and suffocate, not considering the steps involved in how this would logically occur. I needed a great deal of help in developing rational thinking despite the fact that I was an excellent student, particularly in science.

To address my fear of a child hiding in a suitcase and suffocating, my Uncle Joey asked me how a kid would do that and still zipper the suitcase. He explained that when you zip up something, the latch of the zipper is on the exterior part of the item. So, for all practical purposes, it would be impossible for a child to zipper himself in a piece of luggage and suffocate from a lack of air, when his hand is on the outside of that same luggage.

As far as my fear of my children crawling into the washing machine was concerned, my uncle also pointed out that the agitator of a top loading machine takes up a great deal of room, so a child would probably not be able to fit into it. A front-loading machine has a latch that has to be closed from the outside. Washing machines will not operate with the top or the front door open. So again, my fear was unfounded.

I had a fear that my children could stick a finger in an electric pencil sharpener resulting in an amputation. My uncle spoke to me in the following fashion; "If a child really did put his finger into a sharpener, he would hear a noise. The noise alone would prompt a child to remove his finger. In addition, he would experience instant severe pain, enough for a reflexive action to take place, causing his finger to be removed instantly. That would be the worst-case scenario. Secondly, when operating a pencil sharpener, the object has to be inserted fairly deep into the machine. This depth is probably greater than a child's finger. Thirdly, the sharpener is not a guillotine. It is not sharp enough to cut off a body part." By the way, have you ever heard of a child losing his finger in a pencil sharpener? I haven't. With my uncle's help, I was able to overcome yet another irrational fear.

As time passed, I practiced logical thinking to combat OCD thoughts on my own. One evening, I was making baked ziti. As I added pre-purchased tomato sauce to the dish, I noticed some "black particles" on top of the ziti. Right away, I became very concerned about the safety of these black particles. My anxiety level started to rise dramatically since my mind was racing, conjuring up the following scenario:

> "What are those black particles? Are they some sort of mold or poison? What if I serve my family the ziti and these particles make someone sick? Where could they have come from?"

I looked inside the tomato sauce jar and saw a couple of the same black particles that were on the ziti. I then started reading the label and saw that spices were among the ingredients listed. So, I reasonably concluded that the particles were part of the ingredient list in the sauce and not dangerous. I served the ziti to my family and it was delicious.

Another time, I banged two Pyrex glass dishes together by accident while taking them out of the dishwasher. Right away, I suffered from the "what if" syndrome:

> "What if some glass fragments ended up in the Pyrex dish as a result of the bang? What if I served food in the dish to my family and someone ingested the glass fragments? What if the glass fragments ripped the digestive organs of a family

member and they needed surgery?"

I felt totally responsible for the possible consequences of my negligence. Right away, I washed the Pyrex dish. Then, I inspected the bottom of it to see if it was chipped, and I noticed some scratches. I ran my fingers over them and felt that they were smooth. That was my first indication that there were no glass fragments, yet I was still uncomfortable, and feared that glass might be present anyway. It then occurred to me to look at another very similar Pyrex dish that I did not bang. I noticed that it had the same type of scratches on its base. I concluded that the scratches on the first Pyrex dish did NOT occur as a result of my careless banging accident. I saw no evidence of glass fragments. By observation and simple reasoning my anxiety subsided.

In each of the aforementioned cases, logic and reasoning was used to challenge my ideas. We can learn to distinguish between what is rational and what is not. We have to exercise our reasoning ability. I used to have terrible fears about harming others by my own negligence. Little by little, I began asking myself, "Is there any justification or evidence for the fear?" This became yet another tool to challenge my OCD.

I have progressed to the point that, unless I have concrete evidence, I try to assume that the environment is safe. When we are afraid of harming or contaminating others or ourselves without any evidence, we can recognize the voice of OCD in our heads and identify it as just another OCD falsehood.

Many people (including myself) with OCD have a fear that they might inadvertently hit someone or something while driving, especially if they hit a "bump" in the road, or if they come close to another object. OCDers are known to return to where the "perceived incident" took place endless times for reassurance that some disaster did not happen. If this describes you, you may ask yourself some of these questions:

- Where's the blood or evidence to support this scenario?
- Did I hear any screams or any noise whatsoever?
- Are there any dents on my car? Remember the dents have to "match" the object you think you hit in shape and proportion.

Before you accuse yourself, you must have reliable and valid evidence.

Examine the Probability of an Event Occurring

I worried that my children would dismember their arms and fingers with my husband's power tools. In order to overcome this fear, it was very helpful to break down the feared consequence into the steps that would logically lead up to the supposed event:

The tools are in the garage, not in the house. My husband has already stored them away as a precaution. Secondly, he uses the tools in the garage, and when he has completed his work, he unplugs them. Our garage door is also locked most of the time. In order for my children to open the garage, they would first have had to find the remote control to open the door, then find the power tool, then plug it in, and finally misuse it while unsupervised.

In their formative years, my daughters had no interest in power tools in the first place. However, even if they were interested in playing with power tools, there were so many steps involved in this scenario, that the occurrence of harm was highly unlikely.

When I thought up catastrophes, I had to learn to ask myself, "Have any of those intrusive thoughts ever materialized?" Mostly likely, they haven't and they never will. If you happen to create a scenario in your mind, do not give the thought reality. We can imagine practically anything and find ourselves guilty. The fact that we imagine it, however, does not make it likely.

I placed a planter with geraniums on my deck. The planter was suspended in a bracket, about 7 feet above the ground. I worried about it falling on someone, although I placed it securely in the bracket. This is what my OCD mind thought at the time:

> "What if a hurricane wind blows it down and it falls onto someone's head? What if that person is scarred for life? How will I live with the guilt?"

A lot of our so-called catastrophes involve many steps, although we may not be aware of this at first. We have to logically think through the scenario and break it down into its components. Then we have to consider the probability of each component. I had to talk back to my "planter" thought for several hours in an OCD episode. After some practice, I considered the sequence of steps involved and this is how I spoke to myself:

> "Is there any evidence for the existence of the thought? My neighbors all have above ground planters, and I have not heard about anyone getting hurt. In addition, suppose the planter is not 100% secure. Suppose a hurricane wind occurs, and the planter is dislodged. A person would have to walk exactly where the planter was being thrown from its bracket. What is the probability that a person is walking outside in a hurricane? (Most people would seek shelter.) What is the probability that he or she

is walking in my driveway during a hurricane? What is the probability that the wind would blow a planter to the precise spot where a person was standing? What is the probability that so many steps would occur simultaneously to produce such an event? For all practical purposes, it is negligible."

Addressing Intolerance for Uncertainty (Grayson, 97)

We can never be 100% sure of anything. Even though the probability of my planter disaster happening is negligible, it is not zero. By the same token, nothing is ever one hundred percent perfect, or one hundred per cent safe. That is true here for everything on earth!

I would like to add, however, there is one thing that is certain, and that there is a Creator, who loves us and forgives us, and eternally gives us the strength to cope with this secular world. Basically, in life, all things are perishable. Money can be gained and lost, your loved ones will leave one way or another, friendships will come and go, and the strength of your body will eventually decline. The one thing that is truly eternal is your relationship with God. No one, except yourself, can take it away from you.

Thoughts are precisely that, just thoughts. Thoughts are NOT events.

In a very angry moment, did you ever think about taking

your child's head (or anyone's head, for that matter) and bashing it into the wall? In my child rearing days, I had thought about it, while in a very emotionally angry state, but had never actually done it. The problem that plagues OCD sufferers is that sometimes they feel that they might act on a violent OCD thought, when in fact, they would not. There is an unrelenting element of doubt; "Would I really do this? Am I a terrible person for thinking this?" Yet an OCD sufferer that may have brutal thought obsessions does not have the personality profile of a criminal.

Ian Osborne, MD, writes in *Tormenting Thoughts and Secret Rituals*, "violent thoughts are normal for the human race, and overly responsible, guilt-prone OCDers are the least likely people to ever act on them." Jonathan Grayson, author of *Freedom from Obsessive Compulsive Disorder*, cites that "studies examining the thoughts of OCD sufferers and non-sufferers have found no difference in the content of the thoughts…any and all thoughts that come into your mind, no matter how evil, twisted, or perverse they seem, are normal."

A Warning: If you actually take decisive action on achieving a detrimental thought, think that hurting or molesting others would be fun, or you hear voices telling you to do such things, this does NOT fall into the category of OCD, and you need to get professional help (Grayson,

210-211).

Trying Not to Think about Obsessive Thoughts Does Not Work

OCDers with mental compulsions become fixated with the fact that they have such thoughts and they try not to think of them. This attempt of trying not to think about the obsession, of course increases the frequency of the thought. If I said to you, "Don't think about the latest violent act just reported in the news," you would have a hard time NOT thinking about it. You cannot make your thoughts go away by fighting them. Dr. Penzel, in his book, *Obsessive Compulsive Disorders: A Complete Guide to Getting Well and Staying Well*, says, "If you want to think about it less, think about it more."

If you have an intrusive OCD thought and you have trouble dismissing it, you can manage the thought by speaking back to it in the following way:

> "This is just another OCD thought like the hundreds of others I've had. What happened to all those OCD thoughts? They eventually vanished. I can't even remember what they were. And this OCD thought, just like the others, will disappear as well."

Remember, the more you trivialize these thoughts, the quicker this mental trash will disappear from your mind.

What is the Worst Thing that Could Happen?

I used to become anxious in the middle of the night, thinking that I might have left a faucet on, wasting water. In my mind, there would be water damage to the house everywhere. I would get up and repetitively check the faucet to relieve the anxiety. My normal course of action is to conserve resources, since I was brought up never to waste. The thought of leaving the faucet on became a catastrophic event in my mind. I eventually learned to ask myself, "What is the worst thing that could happen?" If I left a faucet on, I would, in fact, waste some water. I am not advocating leaving faucets running. But if I made a mistake, it would not be the catastrophic event I used to envision. I had greatly exaggerated the damage that could theoretically occur. In all probability, if a faucet is left on, water is wasted and goes down the drain. Logically, the probability of leaving a faucet on full force is highly remote, because a running faucet is audible, even from an adjacent room. And by the way, had I carelessly left a faucet on and some damage did occur, it could have been easily fixed, and my negligence would have been forgiven.

I have now gained a sense of perspective since my recovery and realize that almost all of my concerns were of a trivial nature. (When I was ill with OCD, however, my fears were certainly NOT trivial to me.)

Do you "Check" Reliably? Reduce your Self-doubt by Logical Argument

Did you ever check something, recheck it, and found that you made a gross error? Usually the answer is an emphatic "NO." **That means that after checking one time, you are dependable and reliable.** Did you ever notice that a door was left unlocked when you were doing routine household chores and NOT involved in a checking ritual? On a couple of occasions, I did observe that my husband or children have left doors or windows unlocked. Guess what I then did! I locked it. And I thought about the following: **if something were unlocked, or irregular, I would notice it, and correct it immediately**. Here was more proof that I need not check something repeatedly. I did not need to have so much self-doubt. If I checked something once, it was enough, since I was dependable. You might ask yourself these same questions and start eradicating doubts about your abilities. Remember that doubt is the voice of OCD speaking to you. Historically, OCD was even named the "doubting disease" (Rapoport, 18).

Every Time You Check, God Checks Too

Nowadays, I do check a window that I have indeed opened, or a door before going to bed, but I check it visually one time on a good day. I make a conscious, mindful effort when I close the door, by listening for the sound when the door is securely in its frame, turning the latch, and again listening for the clicking sound as I do so. I visualize that God is my constant companion and He checks with me. After I leave, I discuss the matter with God, and He assures me that what I was checking is safe and secure. I thank Him for His support and then go to bed in peace.

What Happened Before You Developed your Checking Rituals?

Did you ever notice that your laundry list of checking things was expanding? I started out with checking doors. Before long I added windows. Then the kitchen ritual began. I checked both the oven and gas stove, staring at each of the four gas burners a few minutes. This would have to be done in the light and in the dark. Soon, I began to have doubts about even my visual inspection. So, I developed the following procedure: I would place my hands on each of the burners just to be "extra" sure that I did not leave them on. My doubt still remained, however, so I "improved" my system. After a time, I would place my two hands on the two front burners. I would then take my two hands and place them on the back burners, while placing the back part of my forearms and elbows on the front burners. Does this sound bizarre? It was. It was pointed out to me that I had developed these rituals, but I did not do them for most of my life. Yet somehow, I was able to get by and not burn any houses down for my entire existence, which is now greater than one half of a century. So, I finally realized that if I did not check something before, I did not have to start checking it now.

How to Talk Back to a Fear of Not Sleeping

I admit that my OCD has cost me countless sleepless nights. During the worst times of my life, I developed pre-sleep anxiety where I feared I would not be able to go to sleep at night and might not sleep for days and days. Then I imagined getting into my car, falling asleep at the wheel and killing someone, although I have a good, reliable driving record, and have never fallen asleep at the wheel.

If you are afraid of not breathing, you will not breathe efficiently. The fear of not sleeping caused me not to sleep. Suppose I confided in you, and said, "I have a fear of growing horns on my head. I don't want to have horns – I would rather die than have them on my head." What would you say to me? A reasonable response might be, "That is stupid; you are not going to grow horns on your head." Well, my fear of not sleeping was just as stupid. A way to talk back to a fear of not sleeping is by saying to yourself:

> "Sleep comes naturally when I am tired. There is no reason for me not to sleep. If I don't fall asleep right away, at least I will rest. I have options – I can pray to God, read something spiritual, write in a journal, or think beautiful, kind thoughts. I will eventually sleep in God's embrace. I love Him."

How to Handle the Concern about what Other People Think

I am a people pleaser, prone to feeling guilty. So, of course, I was always concerned about what other people thought. I put a lot of unnecessary pressure on myself worrying about what people would think and/or say if I did not perform as expected or do what I was asked. My worrying extended not only to my job performance, but to my leisure activities as well. For example, I have played tennis for many years, and used to have a fear of losing. I actually worried about it to the point that my game was compromised. What would others say if I lost to "so and so?" My ego was way too big.

One day my uncle and I were casually watching a

Challenge and Analyze Your OCD

couple of adolescent boys playing basketball in the schoolyard. One of the boys was playing especially well. My uncle pointed him out, saying, "Look at that boy. While he's playing ball, he is smiling, and obviously enjoying himself. He is certainly not worried about his performance." I thought out loud, "How many times have I played tennis and NOT enjoyed myself because I was concerned about the score, losing, and what people would say?" I decided that I would be better off losing, but enjoying myself, and smiling like the boy in the schoolyard. From then on, I changed my goals, and tried to laugh on the court and have fun. I no longer tried to be "number one" and made a conscious decision that my shots need not be perfect. In fact, I developed the attitude that I could lose 6–0, play well (according to my ability) and still enjoy the workout.

The same attitude also carried over to any performance related activity. What would people think if I screwed up? When I taught, I was worried about being observed by my supervisors (and colleagues) should they walk into my classroom and be disappointed in the lesson. I would have a great deal of pre-anxiety if I knew that an outsider would visit for evaluation purposes. I am now in a different work environment, but I am more relaxed about "being observed." I still try to be diligent, by preparing, and doing an appropriate, but not perfect job. If the evaluator is not satisfied with my performance, I am willing to take constructive criticism and make attempts to improve. However, I say to myself, "Do I really care what this person thinks of me? She is only an EARTHLY person. What is really important is that God loves me unconditionally and approves of me, merely because I am His child. I do not have to try to please Him." Secondly, I am making assumptions that what others are thinking is negative. Unless I have direct evidence, I will try not to assume that. My employer, supervisor, peer, etc. is also a child of God; I will be respectful, self-reflective, and try to improve for everyone's benefit in order to perform to the best of my ability. If I do all of the above, and I still receive a negative evaluation, I consider myself a work in progress, and leave it at that. I will not over-react to harsh words when I have what is truly important – a spiritual lifestyle.

Surprisingly (or maybe not so surprisingly to you) my performance in many aspects of life has improved. That was my reward for the appropriate thought selection and attitude.

Address your OCD Thoughts

Think of your OCD thoughts as if they were mosquitoes. They might surround you. Once in a while, one of them bites you. That is okay; it is not fatal. The more you master OCD thoughts, and talk back to them, the easier they are to get rid of. What happened to your other OCD thoughts? They disappeared. So, will this one. Be patient.

You may also address an OCD thought by saying to yourself, "I know what is happening, and I am prepared for you."

At the first twinge, fight back by answering the thought in your mind. The earlier you prepare and challenge the thought, the quicker it will leave. An acquaintance of mine talks to her thoughts this way:

> "Hello, OCD thought. I am glad you dropped by. When are you leaving?"

How I Try to Lead my Own Life and What I Try NOT to DO

I don't watch violent, horror, or murder mystery movies mainly because they upset me. The power of suggestion is, as I mentioned before, very powerful. I don't need any more material to fuel figments of my imagination, especially disasters and catastrophic events. If it is not funny, informative, or inspiring, I don't want to see it. My husband and children understand that, when they are watching something I don't want to see, I have to get up and walk out of the room.

I don't drink alcohol, coffee, or caffeinated

products. I am energetic, and anxiety-prone, and the last thing on earth I need is a stimulant.

To a large extent, I don't make up the imaginary, creative disasters in my mind any more. I also try NOT to dwell on or embellish angry, jealous, or bitter thoughts and do my best to dismiss them. It is important to be mindful of your thought-life and try to eradicate the mental trash.

What I Try to DO

I like to exercise. I enjoy playing tennis, bike riding, walking, and gardening. Gardening, in particular, strengthens and improves the body, calms and clears the mind, and brings joy and caring to the soul, especially while observing some plants growing, flowering and producing an edible harvest. Whether I am focusing on my tennis swing, or digging in my yard, I concentrate fully on what I am doing, and I do not have a care in the world. According to Dr. Stephen S. Ilardi, author of *The Depression Cure*, there are over one hundred studies, which demonstrate that exercise is a natural anti-depressant; it increases the activity levels of serotonin, the same neurotransmitter targeted by the SSRIs (14).

I do read spiritual, inspirational material. Some suggestions, which I have personally enjoyed, are:
- The New Testament
- The Shack

- Dare to Forgive
- Inner Peace
- Put the Past Behind You and Give the Gift of Forgiveness
- A Gift of Love: Reflections for the Tender Heart
- Becoming Emotionally Whole
- Achieving True Contentment and Purpose: Success God's Way
- Fearfully and Wonderfully Made
- With God All Things Are Possible: A Handbook of Life
- God, Faith, and Health: Exploring the Spirituality – Healing Connection
- A little spiritual publication called the "Daily Word"

I believe that we should make an attempt to live by showing compassion, caring and love to our fellow human beings. I do want to try to reduce the suffering in this world from OCD; this is the primary reason for my writing this book. I know firsthand how much needless pain is caused by obsessive-compulsive disorder.

I do keep busy and try to lead an active life. It keeps my mind out of trouble. Remember, freedom from OCD, and any illness for that matter, is a very big deal. Once you are free, you will have more time on your hands, since you will not be wasting time on compulsive checking, rituals, and unproductive, obsessive worrying. How will you fill your open moments? Ask God this question and He will guide you.

Dr. Barry Sears mentions in his book, *The Anti-Inflammation Zone,* that the Japanese people have the greatest longevity (without disability) and the lowest rates of depression in the world (39). He attributes this to their diet of fish and other marine animals, and large quantities of fruits and vegetables. I do try to maintain a healthy diet by eating several servings of fruits and vegetables and taking vitamin and fish oil supplements daily. I eat very little red meat, and I have explored a whole new world of good tastes, including beans and tofu, whole grains, whole wheat pasta, and bulgur wheat. I always loved eating junk food, such as cookies, ice cream and sweet treats, but am trying to keep it to a minimum. I do indulge myself with a treat, such as dark chocolate or some ice cream on weekends or at social gatherings.

There is a program followed by Alcoholics Anonymous in which afflicted people go through a 12-step process in order to give up drinking and maintain sobriety. These same 12 steps exist for Obsessive Compulsive Anonymous (OCA), an organization dedicated to help sufferers defeat their compulsions. The Twelfth Step is described in the OCA book: "Having had a spiritual awakening as a result of these steps, we tried to carry this message to those who still suffer from OCD and to practice these principles in all our affairs." I am lucky enough to have had such a spiritual awakening, and now I try to use my abilities to help others. When you overcome your battle, share your experience and inspire those around you.

Conclusion

Buddha said, "He who conquers himself is a greater warrior than he who conquers a thousand men." The real challenge in life is not to try to change others, which is often almost impossible, or to control external circumstances (which is also many times not possible). Our real challenge is to confront our fears, change our thoughts, and control our emotions so that we can be "masters of ourselves so that we can be servants to others."

This idea is reflected in the poem, "Invictus," written by William Ernest Henley in 1875 (Stanzas 1 and 4 are quoted here).

> Out of the night that covers me,
> Black as the pit from pole to pole,
> I thank whatever Gods may be
> For my unconquerable soul.
> It matters not how strait the gate,

> How charged with punishments the scroll,
> > I am the master of my fate:
> > I am the captain of my soul.

10

You Are Destined for Peace

OCD falls in the category of the obsessive-compulsive spectrum disorders, along with generalized anxiety disorder (GAD), anorexia nervosa, hoarding, hypochondriasis (a worry that one has a medical illness despite medical evidence to the contrary), trichotillomania (hair pulling), and body dysmorphic disorder, (abbreviated BDD, an obsessive concern about minor facial or body defects) (Grayson, 236). Many people that have OCD also experience panic attacks and generalized anxiety. To suffer from anxiety is a tortuous event, to say the least, and I can attest to this from personal experience. At one time in my life, had I theoretically been given a choice of arm amputation in order to relieve my anxiety, I would have told a doctor, "Go ahead and amputate." Yes, it was that bad.

During an earnest conversation with God, I pleaded for peace. I promised Him that if I could attain the peace that passes all human understanding, I would devote my life to Him. Now I have my precious peace for the overwhelming majority of the time and am on no anti-anxiety medications. For me, the attainment of serenity has been a greater achievement than obtaining any degree, career, relationship, or material possession. If you choose to make peace your number one priority, you too can attain it. It will require perseverance on your part, but then what worthwhile goal does NOT require effort?

Make a Choice to Trust God and Surrender to Him

People with OCD are classically rigid and inflexible. We want to control our environment and try to make everything as risk free as possible to prevent some imagined catastrophe from happening to either ourselves or our loved ones. We attempt to control circumstances, so that we can be free of anxiety. As I stated earlier in this book, I used to worry when my daughter stayed out until the early hours of the morning at the tender age of eighteen. I demanded that she come home early, before all her friends did, because I could not sleep until she returned. In my quest to control things, I gave both of us a great deal of grief. I had to learn the hard way that it is difficult to control the behavior of a young adult. I wanted her home, not so much for her benefit, but for my own peace of mind so that I could relax and finally stop worrying.

I once asked my wise uncle, "What can I do to control my daughter's behavior?" His answer was, "She can vote, get married, and basically do what she wants. You cannot control her behavior anymore, NOR SHOULD YOU. You must love her unconditionally, just as God loves you. You may advise her if she asks you. Have a reasonable discussion about what time she expects to be home. Do NOT give her a specific curfew, however." This message stuck. After many heated discussions I finally said, "You are obviously going to attend these late-night gatherings. How are you getting home? I would appreciate a cell phone call letting me know where you are, not because I want to monitor your life, but I want to know where you are in case of an emergency. When you walk through the door of our home, can you just text me so I know that you are safe?"

Over the course of time there was less discord about when she would come home. My daughter began to comply with my wishes. The sleepless nights and my worrying about her late-night outings largely disappeared. My daughter matured and let me know her whereabouts, and her approximate arrival time home, by texting. My role is now to give her the best guidance possible to make reasonable judgments. Beyond that, there is nothing more I really can or should do. She became a grown-up and needed to learn to make her own decisions without parental regulation.

If you feel the need to control the behavior of other adults, give up your desire for control and surrender to God. We can control very little in the outside world, and that includes the actions of our children beyond a certain age. The only thing we really have control over is our own actions, reactions, and thought processes.

We can be confronted with very difficult life situations, such as the loss of a loved one, marital and family troubles, financial problems, and health issues. When we face trouble, we can say to ourselves, "I do not know what to do. I am going to leave this task to God, because I cannot handle it myself. I don't fully understand why things happen, but I am NOT going to lean on my own understanding. In all cases, God is in charge, not me, and I trust Him."

Before you go to bed at night, and then again in the morning, say to God, "I trust in you unequivocally." Mean what you say. Picture a benevolent, compassionate, loving Being in your mind as you talk and turn your troubles over to Him. My friend, Nan Gale DeBlase, expresses this sentiment in her poem:

"I Let Go"

When life seems a burden so harsh on my soul
When no one beside me can lessen life's toll.
When all that I see is so blinded by grief
With no promise of comfort or longed-for relief.

I let go my sorrow and strengthen my love
By letting God's goodness pour down from above.
No longer are troublesome outlooks proposed
As heavenly calmness replaces my woes.

Believe that God is Love (1 John 4:16)

As I stated earlier, my previous exposure to religion left me with the impression that God was punitive. I was told very clearly by my childhood minister that God was going to hold me accountable for every church service I did not attend and every wrongdoing I committed. God was angry, and if I did not conform to a series of beliefs and rules, I was going to be "damned."

I no longer believe that. Forget about the idea of a God who is out to punish us for some wrongdoing. God is a god of grace, which is unmerited love. I believe that God wants us to be healthy, happy and whole, and loves us more than we could possibly imagine.

Recognize God's Purpose for Us

What is God's purpose for us? I believe that our sole purpose in this earthly life is to be an expression of God's love toward others. If everyone really did God's work, and expressed love, we would have heaven on earth. We live in a land of abundance, and God is supplying our needs.

Give up Earthly Patterns and Materialism

We are bombarded with messages from the media every day, basically telling us if we don't use "such and such" product, we are deprived. Normally, we are judged on what type of career we choose, how much money we make, the possessions we have, our social status, and so on. How about redefining our standards of success? Warren Buffet, one of the world's richest men, once was quoted as saying, "Whoever thinks money buys happiness obviously has no money." This principle is also substantiated in the Bible in *Proverbs 11:16 NIV* "Whoever trusts in his riches will fall."

Research has shown that when people initially win the lottery, they are ecstatic. You would think, "Who wouldn't be after coming into a huge sum of unexpected cash?" However, one year later, they are not any happier than before they won the lottery; in fact, they might even be worse off. A sudden influx of unexpected wealth brings with it its own set of problems, such as professional predators, relatives, and long forgotten "friends" coming out of the woodwork like vultures swooping down to catch their prey. Weeks after the win, the "happiness" wears off (CanWest News Service). University of Virginia psychology professor Ted Wilson states, "Winning the lottery tends to have a terrible effect on social relationships. Newly found financial gain can bring jealously from friends and family members. Winners can lose what really matters, the loved ones in their lives."

The more money you win, the better off you are. Right? Wrong! The true irony is that research by Assistant Professor of Law, Paige Marta Skiba from Vanderbilt Law School, shows that people who won between $50,000 and $150,000 in the Florida State Lottery filed for bankruptcy at a 50 per cent higher rate than those who won sums lower than $10,000 three to five years after winning. Coming into significant cash did not solve financial problems for the winners, since they tended to make poor choices about what to do with it, only postponing financial distress (Hankins, Hoekstra, and Skiba).

Most people fall into a trap of always wanting more, and not being satisfied. The more you have, the more you want. However, the paradox is that the "more" you accumulate, the less effective it is at making you happy. Dan Gilbert, a psychology professor at Harvard University, and the author of *Stumbling on Happiness,* states that "Once you get basic human needs met, a lot more money doesn't make a lot more happiness" (Futrelle).

In the *Old Testament of the Bible, in Exodus 20:3*, it says, "Ye shall have no other Gods before me." This is, in my opinion, good advice. In essence, we are being told everything "earthly" is unimportant compared to our relationship with God. Many times, we compromise this relationship by giving many other "gods" our time and attention such as money, power, status, and things. The true God is actually last on our list. This is when we act according to our own human nature. Unfortunately, by pursuing earthly matters first, we give ourselves a great deal of stress and rob ourselves of the peace that God so freely offers. If we really want true peace that is independent of circumstances, we must pursue a relationship with Him first and foremost. How can we do this? We must pray, communicate, and think about Him. God will help us minimize the importance of earthly concerns and help us change our value system.

    The graveyards are full of people who were wealthy, yet on their deathbeds had regrets about plowing their efforts into material achievement. People have regretted not spending enough time with their families or developing loving relationships. Few people would say, "I wish I would have spent more time at the office." Instead of being concerned about earthly treasures, we need to treasure God's children and develop warm human connections, whenever and wherever we can.

    Once you have reinforced your relationship with God, and have made it your number one priority, serenity follows more or less automatically. You will be less concerned with what earthly people think about you when you know that there is a God who loves you unconditionally. Material acquisitions and status are no longer your yardsticks. You develop a new set of godly and fulfilling values.

How about selecting NOT to let earthly events influence you to any great extent? You have a choice to make about what really matters, earthly things or spiritual things. Decide once and for all who is master of your life. If you achieve a close relationship with God, you are very successful indeed because you are, in effect, choosing tranquility and contentment.

Live in the Present

There is quite a bit of wisdom in the *New Testament of the Bible* when Jesus says in his Sermon on the Mount: "Therefore do not worry about tomorrow, for tomorrow will worry about its own things. Sufficient for the day is its own trouble" (*Matthew 6:34*). The past is ancient history. The future is unknown. You really only have the moment. Focus your attention on the task at hand and enjoy that moment. Rejoice that God has given you a new day. You can be anxious this minute yet have peace one minute from now. If you do have serenity currently, thank God for feeling well. Do not project into the future and contemplate a negative "what if" scenario. Enjoy watching that sunset, smelling the beautiful scent of a flower, and preparing a meal. Practice focusing on your present activity, so **you can live in the moment** (Seppala).

Recognize that Life is only a Passing Phase

I have been told that I am a very serious person, and that I should be more cavalier about life. I was very solemn about my job, family responsibilities, finances, church duties, and even leisure activities such as playing tennis. Someone once asked me what I did for pleasure, just to relax, and I could not think of anything. I am now trying to "lighten up," and laugh more. I am now getting pleasure out of the simplest of things, such as having a nice conversation with my family members, eating lunch with a friend, writing this book, going for a walk, spending time with dear ones, helping those in need, working in my garden, doing yoga, and praying. There is no permanence to life here on earth, so we may as well make up our minds to enjoy whatever time we are given.

Get Rid of Anger and Jealousy

When you recognize the Holy Spirit or God within, you can express what He represents. Qualities of love, joy, peace, forgiveness, compassion, courage and patience come from God. Anger and jealousy are toxic emotions that are created by YOU and are not spiritual. Recognize the God within you and express Him. This is what leads to true peace and happiness.

I used to be jealous of people who had more acquisitions, professional education, and status in life than me, even though I worked very hard and received better grades. I envied people with exuberant personalities and a sense of humor who had more friends than I did and became angry when I would try to befriend someone and it was not reciprocated. I created mental scenarios where I could get my revenge, surpass them in some way, or make them pay for hurting my feelings. But who really suffered from these ill thoughts? It was me, and no one else. Thoughts of envy, bitterness, and anger are incompatible with a peaceful mind, so you are better off trying to dismiss them (Stanley, 76). I recommend not dwelling on scenarios of revenge or ill will in your mind, even if you would never act on them. I ask God to help me release my venomous thoughts; He does not deny my noble request. Nothing in this world is more precious than tranquility, and a thought-life filled peace, compassion, and caring.

Enjoy God's Creation

I once went on a ski vacation with my good friend Judy and her family. She was not very skilled since she skied only on the "beginner" slopes. I questioned her about this, since I would be unhappy being "stuck" on a beginner's trail all day. She explained to me that she skies to relax and advancing to the next level is not important to her. She enjoys the trail and takes her camera to photograph the ice crystals on the evergreen trees and the beautiful scenery around her. Here was someone who stopped to "smell the roses" and enjoy what she was seeing at the moment. I was so busy worrying about mastering a new challenge that I did not enjoy the skiing the way my friend did. She took full advantage of the gorgeous view and was in no hurry to race down a hill. Her perspective gave me pause; there were great benefits to her way of thinking.

Your Attitude Should be Gratitude

Most of us have quite a bit for which to be grateful. When we are happy for what we have instead of angry or disappointed about what we don't have, we benefit ourselves. Remember to thank God for your blessings on a daily basis. The more often you do this, the better you will feel. You might even make a list and write down all your blessings so that every so often, you can review it. As I previously stated, when you occupy your mind with thanks, you cannot occupy it with other negative ideas, since your mind is capable of only one thought at a time.

When I felt anxious during OCD episodes, I would tell myself, "Yes, I am a little jittery, but I am honestly grateful that it is not worse. I am better now than I was just a couple of hours ago." During the beginning of my recovery, I had to "fake it till I made it." In other words, I may have not totally believed my own self-talk, but I kept repeating it to myself until I eventually did. Being grateful for any small gain at all supports emotional well-being. And small gains over time amount to a big end result. You can tell yourself, "A little is a lot."

I cannot emphasize enough how important it is to look at the bottle half full rather than half empty. I used to dread "getting old" and thought it was a terrible curse. Yet, if I were to admit this to a younger person who had a terrible and terminal disease he would probably say, "You are so lucky; I wish I could get old."

I created a list of my blessings and found that it was quite extensive. Here are a few of the most precious:

- My uncle, husband, children, and all those dear to me
- A developing relationship with God
- His forgiveness
- My progress in attaining emotional well-being and peace
- The realization that the spirit of God is in everyone, without exception
- Having the confidence to heal with God's help

Remember the saying, "I cried because I had no shoes until

I saw a man who had no feet." Count your blessings; appreciate what you already have.

Work Hard on your Spirituality

When I faced my battle with OCD, I began to confide to my skiing friend, Judy, (who by the way, is also very spiritual) about my illness. I had a great deal of doubt as to whether or not I would recover. She reflected on the past and reminded me when she had problems with her teaching job and received a poor evaluation from her supervisor. She was so distraught she needed to seek therapy and was even put on an anti-anxiety medication for two months knowing that she would be closely monitored in the future and her supervisor would be walking in her classroom without prior notice. Many months later she showed me a glowing letter from the same supervisor stating that her performance was much improved; she was a hardworking and dedicated educator, whose students seemed very happy while in her class. My friend beamed with pride as we read her wonderful letter of praise together. She went further, and explained WHY she had shown it to me, saying, "If you work hard enough on something you will achieve it. I worked hard at my job, putting in 60 hours per week at times. If you work hard at getting well, you will overcome your OCD." She was right. I am proud to say that I worked hard to become spiritual and have made great strides in obtaining the peace I desperately wanted. I put in full-time effort, by challenging my negative OCD thoughts, battling for mind control, trying to limit my checking, counting my blessings, recognizing my Divinity, changing my value system and applying spiritual principles.

Addressing my Fear of Death

I can honestly say that I am no longer afraid of my own mortality. **Life is a terminal illness**. Each day that you live means you have one less day here on earth. That is a natural part of our life cycle. We can mentally die a thousand deaths before we actually die. Why should we fear it? Life is a journey that we should learn to appreciate and enjoy.

All living things have a life cycle, which includes birth, life and death. When we die, we decompose because other organisms are able to derive nutrients from our bodies. This is a normal part of the ecological systems we are part of. My own demise means that I am freeing up space and resources for the next generation of people who are entitled to live their lives. When I die, I hope that I can unite with the Supreme Being in some way. However, I don't live to please God to get a "heavenly reward" or an afterlife. I please God because I believe that "God is Love." I can live with uncertainty about the afterlife. I think that God wants us to help others while living here on earth and the fact that we practice love is the reward itself.

You Can Have Peace Regardless of Circumstances

Life is filled with twists and turns, ups and downs, and periods of happiness as well as suffering. God's wish for us is tranquility, and He is constantly offering it to us. There are many biblical references to peace, which many of us crave. In *John 14:27*, we are promised serenity. It says, "Peace I leave with you. My peace I give to you. Let not your heart be troubled, neither let it be afraid." What this passage means to me is that when we give our troubles to God, He replaces it with His peace. God's peace is beyond comprehension because it makes no sense – the circumstances seem to require anxiety, but instead we feel serenity.

While in college, my daughter did not remember to call on her father's birthday, and I was fuming for more than 24 hours, at what I perceived as my daughter's inconsideration and self-centeredness. I also became very angry and sharp tongued when members of my family did not wish to attend church with me. Many times, I wished to attend social events, which gave my husband stress. He preferred his solitude. I badgered him to accompany me, and when he grudgingly complied, he was miserable. As a result, he went home early without me and I would get very upset. There were many years I allowed external circumstances to deprive me of peace. However, once I tried to become more spiritual, by respecting the wishes of my family members, and attending both social and church events on my own – knowing that it would relieve tension, things changed, and I became much less reactive.

    A while after my recovery, my husband was in a car accident in which he was rear-ended. The driver who hit him never pulled over to evaluate my husband's condition; he just left the scene of the accident. My husband was unable to record the license number. When I heard the news, I was able to react calmly and make the appropriate calls to doctors and several collision places. My husband was alright, for which I was extremely grateful, and we eventually got the car fixed at our personal expense. Although it was an injustice that the driver responsible for the accident left the scene illegally, I did not have lingering anger, which I would have had in the past. I was able to focus on the well-being of my husband, rather than the damage to our car. I also realized that God's peace was within me, even during adverse circumstances.

    I believe that the peace we desire is already within us. We only have to bring it to the surface. In fact, God does not approve of worrying about stupidity. He wants us to have reverence for His spirit, which dwells within us.

This place inside us where God resides is not far away. We can go to our inner sanctuary at any moment and have a conversation with Him.

When spirituality is truly practiced, you will find that the emotions of fear and peace have very little to do with external circumstances. Ella Wheeler Wilcox expresses this sentiment in her poem:

"'Tis the Set of the Sail"

One ship sails East,
And another West,
By the self-same winds that blow,
'Tis the set of the sails
And not the gales,
That tells the way we go.
Like the winds of the sea
Are the waves of time,
As we journey along through life,
'Tis the set of the soul,
That determines the goal,
And not the calm or the strife.

I love this poem because Wilcox emphasizes that calmness is attainable even during the stormy times in our lives. I used to believe that everything had to be going my way for me to have peace. I now realize that premise is false. By recognizing the Divine within, you can have peace regardless of your circumstances. "He who is within you is greater than the world." I still am subject to earthly influences and become fearful and a little guilty once in a while, but generally speaking, I am much more at peace than I ever was.

This same offering of peace is available to you. All you really have to do is accept and embrace God within you. You can have peace knowing that He is with you every moment, and that you are unconditionally loved. This knowledge brings true, permanent peace. Work toward becoming a spiritual being and you too can succeed at overcoming your anxiety and OCD and achieve the "peace that surpasses all human understanding."

11

Medication and My Experience with It

When my children were small, and it was obvious to my husband that I had a problem, he tried to help me by printing out some literature on OCD and asking me to read it. I was certainly not ready to admit to having a mental illness, so I became very upset, cried, and called my uncle, screaming into the phone, "I don't want to have OCD." After a time, however, I suspected that my husband might be correct, so I began to discuss my problems with my uncle. He was a very empathetic and compassionate person to everyone, so I felt comfortable bearing my soul to him. However, I would discuss my symptoms with no one else, since I felt very ashamed and made every attempt to conceal them. It took a while for me to even admit my fears to my own husband. I perceived my illness as a character flaw; it was my own fault and thought that I should be able to handle my weaknesses on my own. In addition, I did not want to be stigmatized as mentally ill; after all, who would?

Of course, when an underlying problem is not addressed, many times, it gets worse, which is exactly what happened in my case. When my OCD fears peaked, I became very anxious and depressed, finally conceded to medical help, and started seeing a psychiatrist. I also confessed my emotions to my minister at the time and asked him, "If I were to harm myself, would I still be a "child of God?" I will never forget the minister's words – He said, "What you have is biochemical. You will always stand right with God." He asked me if I was on an antidepressant. I told him that I had been on a very low dose of Paxil (an antidepressant) for a short time. He said that I needed to reach a therapeutic dose, as well as some patience until it "kicked in." He confided that my using such a medication was nothing to be ashamed of; *in fact, he was taking Paxil himself.* I cannot tell you how relieved I was after that conversation. I finally was beginning to realize that my illness was NOT caused by an unhappy childhood, an overprotective mother, or something my family or I did. My self-incrimination decreased and my education about this psychological disorder began as I began going to the library and ordering books about OCD. As I stated earlier in Chapter 2, I came to the realization that OCD is not a character flaw; it is a neurobiological illness (Osborn, 180).

For a very long time, the medical profession had little to offer for the treatment of OCD. About thirty years ago, the reduction of OCD symptoms was observed when certain medications, the anti-depressants, were used. These medications are also referred to as the selective serotonin reuptake inhibitors, or SSRIs. At around the same time, cognitive behavioral therapy was found to be effective as well. Most OCD clinics today offer a combination of these two treatments. To my knowledge, however, spirituality is not incorporated into conventional OCD treatment. My personal opinion is that it is God who is our ultimate healer, and we should never underestimate our own healing power within.

I am a health-conscious person. Since I used to be anxious about so many things, I have avoided medications in general for most of my life, since I feared their side effects and the possibility of addiction. Although I grew up in the 60s and 70s, I never experimented with drugs, which was unusual given the time period. I was initially opposed to taking medication of any kind, even for OCD treatment.

However, in desperation, when I experienced chronic anxiety, weight loss, and severe OCD symptoms, a psychiatrist prescribed 5 milligrams of Paxil. I remember holding the pill in my hand, refusing to take it. I had researched the side effects on the internet, (which I subsequently found is NOT the best way to research a topic), read some "Paxil" blogs containing some negative information, and of course, became very anxious about taking the drug. In addition, I still considered taking medication a sign of weakness. I had to be convinced to ingest it by my usually patient, but exasperated uncle who, over the phone, told me to "take the damn pill already."

Since my chronic anxiety was becoming quite intolerable and I was barely functioning, I gave in and finally swallowed it. That was the beginning of my medication regimen.

Despite all the internet comments I had read about side effects, the only one I personally experienced was a case of dry mouth. This side effect disappeared in about one week. About seven to eight weeks later, the medication was increased to 10 milligrams of Paxil. I was prescribed a relatively small dose, which was increased gradually, so that I was less likely to suffer harsh side effects and that I would not abandon a potentially helpful medication.

A short time after first seeing the psychiatrist, and while on 10 milligrams of Paxil, my symptoms did not abate. I guess that I waited too long to get medical attention, until I was spiraling out of control. My uncle called my husband, very concerned, because I had asked him to help me end my life. By then, my husband, uncle and our families were extremely worried, and realized I needed to be in an environment where I could be monitored. I left my job on a Thursday and wound up in the hospital on Saturday, one day before Easter, on suicide watch. I will never forget the scene where, after my admission, I was placed into a wheelchair, while a police officer pushed me down a hallway, through a series of double doors that locked right after we entered. My perception was that I was now in prison, being constantly watched and told when and what to eat, when to go to bed, and so on. Upon entering the ward, I remember having to give up most of my personal possessions, including a cell phone. My husband gave me a bunch of quarters so I could use a coin phone in a public hallway in order to contact him. My money was taken from me, along with other "unapproved" items. He left, and I spent the night in a room with two other very sick women. The next day, I asked the hospital staff for my money taken from me the previous night, and a staff member told me, "You must be suffering from delusions – you have no money here," and then walked away. At that point, I felt as if I had lost every ounce of my personal dignity. In the next several days, I had to make quite a few adjustments to my new world. Hospital staff "took notes" while observing my behavior, and I would stealthily try to read them before they were concealed. Once, I was able to read, "Patient is walking up and down the hallway, constantly pacing."

Once in the hospital, I was encouraged to socialize and finally did, because I wanted to appear "normal," and leave the psychiatric ward. This in and of itself was a good thing. Concentration was difficult, since intrusive thoughts occupied my mind, and I had trouble focusing on external activities. My medication was increased to 20 milligrams of Paxil during my hospital stay. When the staff psychiatrist asked me if I was sleeping, I responded, "No, it was too difficult to sleep at night in the ward with all the disturbances." I was then given yet another medication, Trazadone, to help me sleep at night.

In hindsight, I was blessed because I had people that cared. I had a roommate who did not have any support. While in the hospital, my husband came to visit every night after work, giving me money for phone calls, which I was then able to keep, reading materials, my gradebooks, student papers, chocolate and whatever else I wanted, subject to the approval of the staff. My uncle and my best friend, Vicky, also came to see me every day. I also became a kind of "point person" for the other patients who would routinely ask me for money and treats, since they found out that I had a good supply. I gave since I felt sorry for the several patients who had no visitors, no money and no contact with the world outside the psychiatric ward. Many of them were more seriously ill than I was. Yet, I was so overwhelmed by my own psychiatric disturbances that I could not fully understand their problems.

After a six-day hospital stay I was able to come home, after the hospital staff no longer considered me a danger to myself. I must say that this occurred with a lot of my uncle's help, after he had a conversation with a staff psychiatrist that had been evaluating me. I received bans on

Medication and My Experience with It

working and driving, and as a result, had a lot of spare time on my hands. The extra time ended up being a huge bonus – I could get therapy and devote myself to healing.

I was told not to drive because I was placed on a drug called Seroquel, an atypical anti-psychotic drug. Once at home, I had a problem getting to different places, since my neighborhood lacked an efficient mass transportation system. I relied on the good will of neighbors and my husband, who would take me food shopping and to the doctor. I never liked being dependent on anyone, so I began bicycling long distances as a means of transportation in order to minimize my impositions on others. My friend Vicky and her partner Hank treated me to many nice restaurant lunches because they recognized my weight loss and wanted to help. My unexpected hiatus from work and responsibility became my opportunity to research my illness and attempt to recover. I purchased a couple of anxiety and OCD books that offered some practical advice, as well as some insight into my own thinking. I also began reading a great deal of spiritual literature for inspiration.

The instructions on the vial of my hospital prescription of Trazadone were to take it "as needed." I decided that I did NOT want or need it. Instead, I committed myself to studying spirituality for several hours a day. About two weeks after the hospital discharge, I saw my private psychiatrist. He increased the Paxil to 30 milligrams and told me flat out that he did not believe in spiritual healing. He insisted that I take the Seroquel, which I was not happy about since it prevented me from driving, and also prescribed another medication, Ativan, which I really objected to.

Ativan falls into a group of antianxiety medications that are sometimes prescribed in OCD treatment known as the benzodiazepines (BZDs). This group includes chlordiazepoxide (Librium), diazepam (Valium), alprazolam (Xanax), lorazepam (Ativan) and clonazepam (Klonopin). Unlike the SSRIs, this group of medications can be physically and psychologically addicting. Physicians may prescribe them if the patient experiences severe anxiety and panic attacks, and/or severe, disabling OCD symptoms. These medications do relieve anxiety, and address symptoms, but I was afraid of becoming addicted from taking even one pill. I personally did not want to start with such a medication to treat symptoms – I wanted to attempt to get at the root cause of my problem instead. Later on, I realized that addressing my thought patterns were necessary in order to achieve my ultimate goal of OCD and anxiety recovery. In hindsight, I can certainly understand why a person would take such a medication, having experienced chronic anxiety myself. It is a terrible feeling, and it was a major contributory cause of my hospitalization. At the time, however, I had severe objections to it, and my doctor refused to discuss my fear of addiction, saying that I only would be on it temporarily, and he would not "let me" become addicted. Because he shut down certain conversations – such as my pursuit of spirituality, and my fear of addiction to Ativan, I had little faith in him and realized that our doctor-patient relationship was deteriorating.

I was still highly anxious, however, and had OCD symptoms and compulsions. One highly beneficial aspect of spare time after my hospital release was that I began journaling my feelings on a regular basis. One day before my younger daughter's sixteenth birthday, at about 4 PM in the afternoon, I began to ponder a statement made by my uncle: **"OCD is a disease of false fear and false guilt."** I thought to myself: **"Could all my fears be one big hoax**? Could my guilt really be misguided? Could my entire problem be self-induced?" The words started to register, and during an aha moment I began to view my fear and guilt as potentially being false. Over the course of two hours, as I started to "see the truth," my anxiety level began to decrease on its own. It was as if I had a miracle healing – veracity was setting me free. I experienced a peaceful night. The following morning, I looked at the bottle of prescribed Ativan in my medicine cabinet and realized I could function without it. I was not that anxious. The next day, my anxiety levels continued to decrease further. I was healing and getting well without the Ativan, due to my new metacognitive awareness. My fears were abating. God was healing me, and each day, I began trusting Him more and more.

About a month later, I was still on 30 milligrams of Paxil, and 50 milligrams of Seroquel, which has numerous side effects, once of which is to make a person drowsy. However, it did not make me drowsy in the morning at all. I learned that if a side effect is present in even one person, it must be listed in the medical literature. When I explained the absence of this side effect to my psychiatrist, he gave me "permission" to drive and I was able to resume an important function in my life for both myself and for my family. My health was progressing. I then created a new immediate goal for myself – to get off the Seroquel completely.

I basically wanted to take as little medication as possible for several reasons. First, I wanted to explore spirituality and depend on God for my healing. Second, two months after hospitalization, I began experiencing, restless leg syndrome whereby I felt very unpleasant, tingling sensations in my legs and feet, especially at bedtime, which kept me awake at night. I visited a neurologist who found no biological basis for the sensations. I believed the tingling to be a residual side effect of the medication, since I did not have restless legs

Medication and My Experience with It

before I took the Paxil or the Seroquel.

My ultimate goal was to be off medications altogether. Unbeknownst to my psychiatrist, I eventually reduced the Seroquel gradually, thinking that I would not have to deal with side effects. It was a big blow when he told me, "You will be on medication the rest of your life." When I told him that I had been reducing the Seroquel dosage over time, he balked and became very angry. I suppose that he was justified, since I had eventually eliminated Seroquel without his knowledge. However, I did not feel that my doctor was encouraging, willing to listen to what I had to say, or that we shared common goals. Alternative methods of healing and spirituality were off limits for discussion. I felt in my heart that spirituality would address the fear and guilt, so fundamental to OCD.

I needed some paperwork that required a physician's signature in order to receive an extended medical health leave for my full-time teaching job. My principal was gracious enough to offer me over a year's time in order for me to recover and come back to work. However, my psychiatrist refused to sign and did not give a valid reason. I am guessing that it was because I was not compliant with his medication regimen, and this was a way of saying he no longer wanted me as his patient. I remember walking out of his office upset and shaking, realizing the consequences – losing my own medical insurance, pension plan, and career. This was a huge blow to my ego, and had I been alone, the consequences would have been detrimental. It is terrible to have your career terminated in one day. In addition, I had no desire to continue as his patient – we were obviously not a good match from the very beginning.

Yet God works in mysterious ways. I was able to find a new psychiatrist, covered by my husband's medical insurance, in a relatively short period of time. He was open minded and respectful of my wishes to make me, himself, and God part of our medical team. We are still together after many years. After being forced to resign from my full-time teaching job, I was not under any time pressure to recover. I could continue exploring spirituality and continue my rehabilitation. Four months after hospitalization, I was still on 30 milligrams of Paxil with restless leg syndrome symptoms, reaching a therapeutic dose. My checking obsessions and compulsions were decreasing by leaps and bounds due to the medication regimen, my newfound spirituality and an evolving, (and much healthier) thought process.

I must admit that my restless leg symptoms were annoying – the tingling and pricking sensations in my legs would not subside until I moved my legs. I was tossing and turning for hours at night until I was able to fall asleep. It was difficult to get up in the morning with such an erratic sleep schedule, making the possibility of full-time work a questionable proposition.

I read that after a while on a therapeutic dose, a physician might reduce the medication gradually, and ask the patient about the severity of symptoms. This is the maintenance phase of treatment. A patient may be able to get along very well on a lower maintenance dose of the SSRI after the acute phase of OCD is over.

I discussed the restless leg symptoms with my new psychiatrist and asked for a reduced dosage of Paxil, hoping to reduce this side effect. He agreed to cut the dosage to 20 milligrams per day. After a few months, I asked for still another reduction, and he lowered the dosage to 10 milligrams per day. However, I still had restless leg syndrome and complained again. In my innermost heart, I probably was still intent on eliminating medication all together, and "beating" the illness on my own. My doctor was hesitant about this and advised against it. He suggested switching to another SSRI drug – 25 milligrams of Zoloft.

Unfortunately, at about the same time my medication was switched, my dear uncle was diagnosed with lymphoma. If that were not enough, my daughter started to show signs of mental illness in college that were interfering with her academic studies. Compulsion behaviors were no longer an issue; however, the irrational fear, anxiety and intrusive thoughts came back in full swing. My thought life regressed to old patterns. Fortunately, I was not hospitalized, since I had the proper medical and family support structures in place. For the next two months, the Zoloft was steadily increased to 150 milligrams per day. My psychiatrist explained that stress was at least partially responsible for my relapse but assured me that I would recover. I believed his kind and helpful reassurance. Progress became evident again, and after three very long months, I fulfilled my doctor's prediction. The side effect of the "restless legs" returned off and on as the Zoloft dosage was increased.

I had wondered if I would be on medication for the rest of my life. My doctor warned me that past research studies showed a 90% relapse rate for OCD sufferers who discontinued medication. Yet I read about studies in England which found that a majority of patients are able to discontinue medications if they practiced behavioral therapy faithfully. Recent research also shows that it is definitely possible to discontinue medications, even in severe cases of OCD, if effective cognitive therapy has been applied (Osborn, 100).

After about one and one-half years of feeling well, I again pressed my doctor to experiment with lowering the medication dosage. Gradually, every three months, my dosage was reduced a little bit, and I would observe if OCD symptoms returned. My prescription of Zoloft was consistently lowered from 150 to 25 milligrams per day in 25 milligram intervals every three months. This was far better than my previous stint of weaning myself off Seroquel without medical supervision. Finally, I asked my doctor to take me off medication altogether. He did not agree with my decision, but relented, telling me, "You are an adult, and can make your own decisions."

I was functioning decently for about one and one-half years without any medication whatsoever. By this time, I had returned to work as an educational consultant on a per diem basis for three or four days per week and was able to take care of my family. Life was fairly normal .... until I relapsed again.

At the time of relapse, my mind became tormented (particularly about thoughts of an afterlife for my family) and I endured much suffering to the point where I did not want to live, yet I did not want to die. Hopelessness and despair reigned – I lost my appetite and had a lot of trouble sleeping, concentrating and carrying on a conversation. Again, my mind was held captive by OCD and fear, and I became suicidal.

I returned back to my same, compassionate doctor and was given a 150-milligram dose of a new medication called Luvox (fluvoxamine), another SSRI used to treat obsessive-compulsive disorder, a 50-milligram dose of Seroquel, and a benzodiazepine, Xanax, for short-term use to help regulate my sleep at night.

    Dragging one foot in front of the other, I started to believe that I could recover again if I finally stuck to my medication regimen and trusted in God's ability to help me heal myself. I began to see the truth that would set me free and to believe what God was telling me – that I was His unconditionally loved child. I began to expect good in my life and to stop making up negative catastrophic scenarios in my mind. It became somewhat easier to dismiss intrusive, destructive thoughts. I started to see that my fears were again, invalid and self-generated, and that I had the power to "not generate" them and to stop the horrible thinking. My doctor emphatically stated that I was not to undergo any more experiments. I had to accept the fact that I was going to be on medication for the rest of my life. I did, and to this day, I have not had a serious relapse for the past eight plus years.

    During this time, I was able to somehow still work, albeit under my own terms. My work was project based, and I was given short assignments based upon a school's needs and my own personal schedule. There were days when I went to work anxiety-ridden and sleep deprived. However, thanks to my per diem status I also had the ability to reject an assignment when I did not feel well, decreasing my stress and ultimately supporting my recovery. Due to the stigma that is associated with mental illness, however, I did not offer a true explanation about why I would not take on a new assignment, except to say that I had family obligations, or some other "excuse." Once I recovered, I took on a normal schedule of approximately a three or four-day work week.

Presently, I am on a 100-milligram per day dose of Luvox, a small dose. My doctor and I consider it an "insurance policy" against future relapses. I discontinued the Seroquel over time, again under medical supervision, and took the Xanax for the very short term on an "as needed basis" during my third relapse. I don't want to take any more risks and put my family and myself through more torment, and therefore plan to continue taking the Luvox. I still have some restless leg symptoms but I have learned how to either tolerate or manage them.

I must say a word here about the anticipation of side effects. I used to believe that the side effects of the medication were here to stay. FOREVER. I was prepared to live with it. However, I also tried hard NOT anticipate the leg syndrome every night. Why should I expect to have side effects indefinitely?

My uncle and I observed that my legs felt colder than my other body parts at times, so he suggested increasing the temperature of my legs, particularly at night. I sleep with leg warmers, or sweat pants, which has helped. When symptoms are more intense, I take a very warm bath just before going to bed, and then retire under a down blanket, minimizing any air pockets or skin exposure to a colder environment. During the day, I wear knee socks under pants to maintain body heat. Raising my leg and body temperature reduces the tingling and annoying sensations in my legs, and I am able to get an adequate night's sleep a good deal of the time. I have found that stretching my Achilles tendons before bedtime by standing about two feet from a wall (or bed) and leaning my body toward it with my heels flat on the ground, can also be helpful. I am resigned to living with a few symptoms and am no longer **fixated** with the idea that I have to sleep for a certain number of hours every night. If I am not able to sleep well one night, it does not matter that much; I am usually able to compensate for the sleep loss on subsequent nights. Life is not perfect and living with the side effects of a medication far outweigh the alternative of a recurrent OCD episode.

    Fortunately, I have no other discernable side effects. My obsessions and compulsions are minimal. I have learned to overcome my fears and experience dramatically less anxiety, even during adverse circumstances, remembering that peace comes from within. I am capable of working (about three to four days per week), taking care of my family, and fulfilling my obligations. I also became involved with an inclusive, progressive church whose members care deeply about the issues of poverty, inequality, climate change and social injustice. Basically, my life is normal, functional and most importantly, peaceful, without major recurrent OCD episodes. I am extremely grateful to God that I was able to attain my ultimate goal – freedom from the torture of OCD anxieties and compulsions. I am no longer fearful and do not experience horrible guilt. Every day, I try to develop an attitude of gratitude for my many blessings and try to minimize my few obstacles.

Some Take-Aways

I was extremely fortunate that my personal circumstances allowed me to either not work or work part-time. Many people would not have been able to receive help had they lost their job, insurance, and/or did not have a support system as I did. One of my aspirations is to become more involved with the rights of those with mental health issues.

I would also advise you, dear reader, to listen to your family and friends' advice early on. Do not wait; seek medical help from a qualified mental health professional, experienced and knowledgeable in OCD issues, with whom you can have an honest, trusting and productive relationship.

My Promise to God

I made a promise to God that if I recovered, I would try to emulate Christ, by being kind, loving, generous and helping others as best as I can in some meaningful way. With determination and confidence, I am pursuing my spiritual goals on a daily basis.

12

Cognitive Behavioral Therapy

After I was hospitalized, I was sent to a psychologist for therapy as part of my treatment protocol. I described the following incident to him: I had accidently dropped a glass dish on the kitchen floor, and obsessively worried about the possibility of my dog eating the fragments of glass and getting sick. In an attempt to purge my anxiety, I swept the floor at least twice, followed by a complete washing. Yet, I still wanted to get up in the middle of the night to wash it again, for fear that I did not collect "all" the fragments. In hindsight, my OCD was at work in full force. As I started to get up in the early hours of the morning with the intent of washing the floor again, my husband physically prevented me from leaving our bedroom to do further cleaning. His intent was to allow me to experience that even without further cleaning, our dog would be alright. In that particular moment, however, his reaction did not alleviate my anxiety, nor was it remedial. It just strained our relationship; my husband did not know the best way to handle a wife whose OCD had spun out of control.

After hearing my story, the therapist gave me advice on how to clean more thoroughly, and then I was told that I must have "done something" that was the "real cause" of my guilt. The therapist wanted to explore my entire childhood in order to discover the true cause of my fear. Quite a bit later, I found out that my fear about not getting all the potential glass fragments was not a matter of thorough cleaning; it was a matter of erroneous OCD thinking. I also discovered that such advice was totally against what is currently considered an effective treatment for OCD – cognitive behavioral therapy, or CBT.

Dr. Steven Phillipson, psychologist and OCD expert, has said in his article, "Guilt beyond a Reasonable Doubt," that having OCD is like a pole bent in a wrong direction. In order to straighten the pole out, it must be bent the same number of degrees in the opposite direction. According to OCD experts, years of traditional psychotherapy and exploring the patient's past are generally not effective for OCD. A sufferer must face his fears using a **gradual** approach. The consensus among experts is that cognitive behavioral therapy is the most desirable treatment for OCD sufferers. Osborn considers behavior therapy OCD's best treatment, currently helping up to 80 per cent of those who complete it even more effective than medication (68). Dr. Penzel has called behavioral therapy "a treatment that works" (17), while Dr. Grayson considers it the "core treatment" for OCD (60).

In hindsight, it should have been explained to me

that my intense fear of harming my dog by inadvertently leaving glass fragments on the floor from accidental breakage was irrational; dogs function by smell and are not inclined to ingest glass; the occurrence of harm to my dog was an extremely unlikely event. Secondly, I should have been asked to confront my fear by attempting to "clean less" and thereby minimize the ritual. Thirdly, the therapist should not have made the assumption that I "did something bad" because I told him I felt guilty about a feared consequence that never happened. I became aware that OCD sufferers are extremely guilt-prone and suffer from a great deal of "false" guilt, as I explained in Chapter 6.

Fortunately, I did not continue with this therapist for any length of time. My first experience with therapy was not only ineffective; it could have been detrimental. I am relating this experience because I cannot emphasize enough that any therapist you choose, should you decide to go this route, needs to be specialized, encouraging and knowledgeable in OCD and its current treatment methodologies.

The "Do What You Fear" Mentality

CBT differs from conventional therapy in that the patient must first undergo exposure to what she fears and place herself in that situation long enough so that her fear diminishes. While she is undergoing exposure, the patient must prevent herself from performing rituals. This is called response prevention, because the patient is preventing her "routine responses."

Exposure involves a process known as habituation. "If you expose yourself to the feared situation, the level of fear gradually reduces, until your body gets used to the fear" (Osborn, 68-69). For example, if you are afraid to ride in elevators, you would put yourself in the situation of having to ride in an elevator. If you avoid the situation you fear, you will presumably not overcome it because you are not utilizing the benefits of habituation.

When you are trying to discontinue a ritual, or reducing a checking protocol, you will experience some discomfort and anxiety. However, the long-term benefits of overcoming OCD are so impressive and gratifying that some discomfort is worth the enormous gain that you will experience.

Cognitive Behavioral Therapy – Easy to Say but Hard to Do

What if your fear is so great that you cannot get into an elevator, or discontinue a ritual? I quickly found out that I had to be willing to tolerate the discomfort of anxiety, uncertainty, and guilt in order to battle the OCD demon.

Cognitive Behavioral Therapy

I went to a second therapist who practiced cognitive behavioral therapy and asked his patients to undergo exposure and response prevention. He gave me a stack of forms and asked me to create what is known as a "fear" hierarchy, which is basically a list of one's fears in ranked order, with the most highly feared items on the top, and the least feared items on the bottom. I quickly figured out I would have to confront my fears, my personal misery level would be extremely high, and that it would require quite a bit of strong will and emotional commitment to follow through with this form of CBT. After I looked at the forms, and realized what I actually had to do, I said to myself, "There is just NO WAY I can undergo the exposure therapy." I was so intimidated and fearful that I never went back to the second therapist.

So, how did I recover from my wretchedness? Before I was to undergo exposure and response prevention of any kind, I needed God's help to address guilt, perfectionism, and exaggerated responsibility. Adoption of spiritual principles was first and foremost. When I knew I was forgiven for any mistakes I might make, having God's unconditional love and forgiveness, and knowing I could surrender myself to Him at any time by going to my "inner sanctuary," it became much easier to do what I feared. Had I not become spiritual, I believe that I would still be living in an OCD world, obsessively worrying and suffering.

Anything, (including undergoing behavior and response prevention) is easier when God's love and support is recognized.

Grayson, author of Freedom from *OCD: A Personalized Program for Recovery*, describes a series of very detailed checklists divided into the two categories of obsessive concerns and compulsions (74-91). After much deliberation, I did eventually create a fear hierarchy using Grayson's excellent resource. I became determined to confront my fears, only after I had fostered a connection with spirituality and became more courageous by enlisting God's help.

A partial summary of my own particular fears, obsessions and compulsions included:

Contamination fears:

- Serving my family and friends contaminated food (from ingredients that were "old," or food that had been left out too long)
- Eating fruit or vegetables that may have had soft spots or discolorations that indicated spoilage (I would throw the entire product away instead of cutting out the imperfect part)
- Residual fragments of broken glass or broken dishes that could be "potentially" ingested or stepped on, after accidental breakage

Cognitive Behavioral Therapy

Fears of Harm, Danger or Loss:

- Becoming afflicted with illness (such as Lyme disease) or injury for myself and others, particularly my children
- Accidentally losing control and harming others while driving, particularly if I had hit some sort of "bump" in the road
- Causing harm to others because of my own carelessness
- The falling of ceiling fans on myself or loved ones while we were sleeping, since they were located above our beds
- Concerns about whether my house was "safe" enough for my young children; I worried about whether my children could:
    - Become strangled by wearing a necklace while sleeping
    - Choke on small objects, such as candy, carrots and buttons
    - Strangle themselves with cords controlling window shades and blinds
    - Climb out of their crib because I had "accidentally" forgotten to raise its adjustable side (which led me to endlessly check it)

- The mortality and afterlife of myself, family and loved ones
- That I had somehow (unintentionally), acted unethically, cheated or taken advantage of another person
- Living close to electrical power lines, and the theoretical possibility of getting cancer from the "electromagnetic field"
- Losing important documents, or financial instruments, such as US Savings Bonds, thereby making banking especially stressful

Perfectionist Obsessions: Mental Anguish About:

- Communicating perfectly so that no one could take offense or act immorally after reading or hearing my words
- Following all rules at my job perfectly
- Performing all tasks perfectly to the "nth" degree

Checking Compulsions, which included checking:

- Doors and windows, to make sure they were locked
- Water taps, electrical appliances, stoves, to make sure they were off and/or unplugged
- Items to be mailed, especially checks, since I had a nagging doubt that I may not have put them in the mailbox properly and therefore "lost" them

- Forms and paperwork, for possible errors to make sure I had not done anything wrong or unethical
- Locations that I had driven by, to make sure that I did not hit someone or something because of my own negligence
- The location of valuable items to make sure they were still in their respective places – and they were not missing or "moved"

Protective Compulsions:
- Collecting and removing objects from the environment that could possibly harm others – such as unextinguished cigarette butts found on the sidewalk, etc.
- Calling and texting to find the whereabouts of my daughters to make sure no harm had come to them
- Trying to control and limit the activities of my adult children, so I could rest assured they were "safely" at home
- Asking others, particularly my uncle and husband, for reassurance that things were safe, or if future negative events would occur to me or my children

Once I knew I had God's support, and that He wanted the best for me, the "work" of exposure and response training did not seem so overwhelming, and my progress was steady.... God was my partner in solving problems.

Eventually, the rituals and fears left me almost as much as I left them. I no longer feared making a mistake because I had the blessing of forgiveness. My values changed; I worshipped God, not the external world. I began to like myself and become less self-absorbed. I was God's creation and knew that I was created for a beneficial purpose, which I could now start working toward, since the enormous burdens of guilt and perfectionism were lifted from my shoulders.

Limiting and Eliminating Rituals

My ritual of checking doors, windows, and the gas stove multiple times was done right before bedtime. The thought of a burglary, or a fire and/or gas explosion due to my negligence gave me nightly anxiety. Exposure and response prevention in my case meant having to expose myself to the thought of a possible break-in or fire, while resisting the urge to check repeatedly. The idea was that if I underwent exposure to the feared idea, and resisted my checking rituals often enough, I would no longer be compelled to check these items. Naturally, I did not want to worry at night; I wanted to get rid of the anxieties that were keeping me awake. I began the hard work of exposure and response prevention to get well. My method of locking the door would be to close it after I walked my dog, turn the deadbolt, stare at it to make sure it was turned to its proper position, and then bang the door shut several times to make sure the door was in its frame. Then, I went upstairs to go to bed, but many times I would come down again and repeat the staring and/or the banging. Usually, I would ask my husband to check the door for even more reassurance.

First, I had to stop asking my husband for reassurance. That was okay; I had God's assistance instead. He was now my partner in helping me reduce my rituals gradually. I had to analyze the probability of a break in or fire occurring, which was exceptionally low. Sure, there was a small possibility of such an event occurring, but I was willing to accept the negligible risk. After all, if I were to make a careless mistake such as leaving the door unlocked, that would be all right, since I would be instantly forgiven by my heavenly Father. In addition, I realized that if the door were left unlocked, (as opposed to unopened) the chance that an intruder would test and then discover it unlocked, was still remote.

I modified my ritual. At first, I closed the door, listened for the sound as I turned the lock, stared at the lock for a while, and allowed myself to bang it only a couple of times. I prevented myself from going downstairs after I had retired to my bedroom to check again. This made me anxious so that I could not fall asleep for a while. To tolerate the anxiety, which was intense, I kept a nightly list that detailed the items I had just checked, including the door. If I became anxious about the door, gas, etc. I would just refer to my list instead of going downstairs. When my anxiety eventually decreased, I no longer kept a checklist. When I felt even more comfortable, I reduced my staring time. After several months, I allowed myself to check the door only once.

Nowadays, I close the door, turn the lock and listen for the latching sound, and do no more banging or pushing. I check once or twice, and then go upstairs to bed, with no anxiety.

In my OCD days, I would not even open the back door of the house at all just so that I would not have to check it. This is known as classic "avoidance behavior," whereby an individual simply avoids what they fear which keeps the OCD status quo. It also limits our usefulness. Now I freely use the back door when I have to and do not routinely or compulsively check it, although I may check it ONCE, to see that I have diligently locked it.

Guilt is a cornerstone emotion of OCD. I used to think that if an intruder had entered and committed harm, I would become afflicted with guilt, and the ensuing torment, all because of my own negligence. Now, I believe, if someone were to rob or burglarize us, it is the robber, and not I, who should bear the guilt. After all, it is the intruder who is breaking the law.

At the time that I had intense "fear" of an intruder coming into my home, I also suffered from many other fears. I was checking windows even if I had not opened them. My rationale for this was maybe, just maybe, I opened a window and forgot that I had done so.

I started eliminating checking of windows that I personally had not opened, reasonably thinking that if I did not open them, I was not responsible for closing them. There were other people in my house who were perfectly capable of closing the windows they had opened. I created a new boundary as to what MY responsibility was, and what was someone else's. Now I do not check any windows that I have not opened.

I used to have an intense fear of burning the house down, so I repeatedly checked the gas stove to make "sure" it was off. Electrical appliances were unplugged immediately after use. Later, before bedtime, they were checked again. Now, I check the gas stove ONCE (okay, sometimes twice) before retiring at night, IF I used it during the day.

Normally, if a household member had used a toaster or a coffeemaker, a scenario I would ponder at night, I would have gone downstairs immediately to check that it would be unplugged. I thought a fire could start if I did not check these appliances, and it would be my fault. That was my twisted thinking. When I became motivated to undergo exposure and response prevention, I forced myself NOT to do this. If someone used an appliance and left it plugged in, I would leave it alone. I dealt with the anxiety by asking myself, "How many people leave their toasters and coffeemakers plugged in? Many do. And what are the consequences of their actions? They are fine. How many cases have you heard of where a coffeemaker or toaster burned down the house? None whatsoever."

I decided that I wanted to function like the majority of people I knew, thinking if vast numbers of people are not unplugging appliances after use, then I don't have to do it either.

How to Talk to Yourself and Reduce/Eliminate the Compulsive Checking Using Reasoning

When you feel compelled to check something over and over because you are filled with doubt about whether or not you did it correctly, ask yourself the following question: "When you checked something, left, and returned, did you ever find that you had made a mistake?" I didn't. I used to check the faucets to make sure they were "off" numerous times, despite the fact that to my recollection, I never left a faucet running in my life. When you end up checking something for the third, fourth, and subsequent times, do you ever say to yourself, "Boy am I happy that I checked this?" Or, do you, (like me) have regrets about checking again and again, only to say to yourself, "This is a waste of time." If you return to check something, and it is in the same position as it was the last time, you realize that you are not a negligent person; in fact, you are quite reliable.

You may also check something again because you might not remember checking it. The reason you don't remember checking it is because activities such as locking a door or window or turning off a faucet or gas stove become reflexive acts. People tend to do these things automatically. If something is that reflexive, you can tell yourself that it really need not be checked more than once, if at all.

Inconsistency with Checking Rituals

Dr. Jonathan Grayson uncovered inconsistencies in his patients' ritualizing while treating them in his practice (112). Looking back in hindsight, I had far more rituals before bedtime than during the day. As I mentioned before, I performed my rituals in order to calm myself down, so that I could go to sleep quickly and comfortably. My husband noticed this and he pointed out my inconsistency. He said, "Do you think that things are more 'safe' during the day?" Once I began to understand that my checking was inconsistent, and more about my wanting to get rid of anxiety, as opposed to a real safety issue, I was more willing to limit rituals. At night, I desperately wanted to relax and feel secure, and this desire intensified my rituals. During the day, I was distracted by doing many other things, so my anxiety level was lower. Who was I really checking for and why was I doing it? I was driving myself and everyone around me crazy so that I could decrease my own apprehension.

Finally Seeing the Big Picture

At the height of my OCD episodes, my sense of perspective became vastly distorted. For example, I might have felt very guilty by having stepped on a snail (by accident) that was crawling on a front step of my house, but not have felt at all guilty about doing nothing to help the one billion people on our planet who go hungry every day. Gaining a sense of perspective between the trivial and monumental also aided in my recovery.

When I was totally miserable, I would recall my Uncle Joey's comforting words: "One day, you will laugh at all your fears and the stupid things you did." In hindsight, he was absolutely correct. You might want to write down all of your fears, dear reader, so that one day you can laugh at them, too.

How to Handle Relapse if it Occurs

When my compulsions and rituals began to diminish, I became very sensitive and worried about relapsing. I learned from my OCD experiences, however. Even though I suffer from this potentially debilitating illness, I have the ability to recover. In fact, I did relapse, and I recovered AGAIN. Every time I have suffered, I have recovered. I am becoming better at recognizing my OCD thoughts and analyzing them through practice. You will too!

The Role of Stress in OCD

Without a doubt, stress can exacerbate OCD. Sumant Khanna and his co-workers from India compared patients who recently developed OCD to a matched control group. It turned out that the OCD sufferers had twice as many stressful events, such as sickness and death, as their matched controls at the onset of the illness. Research has also shown that when we are anxious, we are more prone to experience worrisome thoughts (Osborn, 190). My OCD became a life-threatening issue when the stresses of menopause, working full time, and teenage family rebellion all occurred simultaneously.

Osborn recommends that when a myriad of problems such as health, marital, and career troubles occur, become aware, prudent, and use discretion (191). If at all possible, try to attenuate the stress inducing factor(s). I resigned from a full-time career in order to critically address my illness and family issues.

Overcoming a Fear of Fear

Franklin D. Roosevelt said, "The only thing to fear is fear itself." Fear is a state of mind. It is an insidious condition that we allow. If you can approach endeavors with confidence and eliminate fallacious and destructive thinking, there is very little in life that you cannot accomplish. You have the emotions of fear, courageousness, happiness, sadness, envy, satisfaction, and so on within you. Since we have the power of selectivity, we can be discriminatory, and encourage the wholesome emotions. We can choose the emotions that God, who has our best interests at heart, wishes for us.

13

Afterword – My Life Today

I made a pact with God – that if I ever recovered and attained peace, I would devote my life to serving Him. God did not deny my noble request; my recovery was granted. Now it is my privilege to serve God the remaining days of my life. There are many ways to serve God, and nurture our spirituality, but I try first and foremost to be a good mother, wife and friend to those dear to me. In addition, I try to help as many people as I can as opportunities present themselves.

My eldest daughter attended and graduated law school, despite a bipolar disorder diagnosis. I am happy to say that I was able to financially and emotionally contribute to the achievement of her dream job. She is presently working as a prosecutor and has been a primary editor for this manuscript. Her perception and suggestions have been invaluable. My second daughter graduated college with a degree in mechanical engineering and presently works as a plumbing and fire protection engineer for a consulting company. Both daughters are hardworking human beings of whom I am extraordinarily proud.

Throughout my trials and tribulations, I was able to remain married to the same man for over 30 years, and we still love each other. I have maintained friendships with a few very special people that I know more than twenty-five years. Finally, I am now able to be an emotional support person to a friend who greatly assisted me when I was in need and feel proud that I can reciprocate.

Several years after my recovery, my dear uncle passed away, which has been an enormous loss. I try to think of all the wonderful moments we spent together. I was inspired to write this book, in part, to keep his memory, words and keen insights alive, so that they may help others who are struggling.

After I began recuperating from OCD, I was lucky enough to return to a previous job. I am working as an educational consultant for a small non-profit company on a per diem basis serving as an instructional coach for (mostly) novice teachers in various schools. I am very fortunate to have a position that has been conducive to my healing process, since I have less stress and the freedom to schedule my work. I have learned many skills while working there – such as how to be reflective about my job performance, and to be metacognitive. This skill transitioned from the job into the rest of my life, so much so, that thinking about my thinking is a frequent occurrence. I also have learned to be more self-evaluative, and to have a growth mindset, so if I have deficiencies in a particular area, I make attempts to improve.

Afterword

I genuinely feel that my faith in God has set me free, and I am no longer subjected to the slavery of OCD. As I stated earlier, I have not seriously relapsed for over eight years. Practicing spirituality, very simply means to practice the love, peace, and self-control that is already within me (and is within you as well, dear reader). With God's help, it has gotten easier each day. It took about three years of basically full-time effort to confront and educate myself about OCD issues. During this time, I looked forward to going to the library to research pertinent sources for this manuscript. I found the studies about OCD and brain research fascinating – it made me feel like a youthful college student again. Only this time around, it was better; I was a student with a passion for learning about this subject.

An article in USA Weekend, "For Good Health, Write Your Woes," points out that writing about an illness can actually improve your health. I concur. I originally intended to write a book with the expectation that my experience of successfully combatting OCD could benefit others. I wanted to share my battle for mind control so that other people would be inspired to use the same mental tools that I used, because I know they work. However, I ended up also benefiting myself because writing gave me a sense of purpose.

There will be people reading this book who are

struggling with OCD and will succeed in winning the battle against this illness. If you have the extra time, I would encourage you to write down your thoughts and experiences. It is a process that will bring you great rewards, not only in sharing your wonderful story, but in bringing you even greater healing and peace.

I have basically been given a second chance at living and intend to use it wisely. I am making steady progress in overcoming the negative emotions of anger, greed, pride and jealousy and am learning how NOT to react to negativity. My days now are more balanced with peace outweighing fear, forgiveness instead of guilt, and love trumping anger. I also relinquished my attachment to money. The material world no longer has the significance it used to. I feel I have enough money to live a simple, quiet life and have learned to be satisfied with what I have. God has become my primary focus, and I converse with Him whenever necessary.

Osborn points out "that a good strategy for anyone, but especially for OCDers, is to find a creative endeavor, a mission, and be devoted to it 100%." In leading group therapy for OCD, Osborn finds that many of his patients find that their minds are quieted when they are occupied (133). I am a person who likes to be busy by nature and make it a point to keep busy by working (for pay as well as for no pay), nurturing family and friendships, helping those less fortunate than me, and actively pursuing physical activity.

The OCD challenges that I presently face are much less aggressive than they once were and often not noticeable. I try not to exaggerate the importance of a job, since my primary objective is to serve God, by helping other human beings; the paycheck is somewhat secondary. I am no longer overly sensitive to criticism or to what my supervisors think.

I am busy, able to function well, enjoy what I do, and am careful not to overstress myself. Stress has been my vulnerability – and my nemesis; my symptoms increase when I am stressed.

I also have changed my diet, by dramatically increasing the number of vegetables consumed per day, and have reduced my red meat consumption, substituting fish or chicken instead. Whole grains and whole wheat are substituted for the white varieties of bread and pasta. Instead of feeling deprived, I have found that my new eating habits have opened up a whole new world of tastes. I have also reduced my sugar intake, and I eat meals at regular intervals. Gone are the days where I skip breakfast, which now usually consists of unsweetened oatmeal or plain yogurt with fresh fruit. Many of my dietary changes were implemented as a result of reading, *Anti-Cancer: A New Way of Life*, written by David Servan-Schreiber, a physician who became a patient when he developed brain cancer.

Freeing oneself from OCD requires a radical change in thinking. My daughter enjoys music very much; it relaxes her. One day, she played a CD that contained the song, "Defying Gravity" (written by Elton John) from the Broadway show *Wicked*. We enjoyed that song together, and she left the CD in my car. A year later, as I dropped my daughter off at college, I replayed that song and as I listened to it, I thought about changing the title from "Defying Gravity" to "Defying OCD," and altered the words to reflect how one's thinking changes as they challenge this illness. Here are the lyrics that reflect the transformation in my own thinking:

> Something has changed within me
> My thoughts are not the same.
> I'm through with playing by
> The rules of my obsession's game.
> I've changed my way of thinking
> Even when I go to sleep
> It's time to trust my Lord God
> Close my eyes and leap.
>
> It's time to try defying OCD
> I think I'll try to accept uncertainty.

Afterword

Kiss me goodbye – false fear and anxiety
And you won't bring me down.

I'm through accepting limits
Cuz illness says they're so.
Some things I cannot change
But till I try I'll never know.
Too long I've been afraid of
Losing peace, I know I've lost
Perfectionism comes at much too high a cost.

I'd sooner try defying OCD
Gives me too much responsibility
Kiss me goodbye – false doubt and anxiety
You won't bring me down.

I'd sooner try defying OCD
Kiss me goodbye – false guilt and anxiety
I'm going to change my brain circuitry
And you won't bring me down.
Bring me down. Oh… oh…oh.

I learned that happiness is a state of mind. It is not dependent on materialism, achievement, status or external circumstances. I am not easily influenced by the opinions of others. Happiness and peace come from the God within.

My only regret is that I did not start practicing spirituality sooner, but am still in the continuous, unending process of evolving. I consider myself spiritually rich and lucky to finally have mental clarity and to be able to use my energy in new, positive and meaningful endeavors.

Farewell:

There is no shame in having a biochemical disorder—OCD. In fact, there will be benefits you experience as a result of your struggle. If you concentrate enough on your recovery, it will materialize. This "disease" may be an event that gives you strength, perseverance, better character and spiritual development.

14
Sayings Worth Remembering

Diminishing OCD Thought

- OCD thoughts are like mosquito bites. You can be surrounded by mosquitoes, and once in a while, one bites you. Afterward, you dismiss it.
- OCD is a disease of false fear and false guilt. Once you realize that, you are well on the way to being cured.
- If you want to think about it less, think about it more (Penzel, 65).
- The more pain one is willing to endure, the less it is experienced (Phillipson, Steven, Speak of the Devil).

Eradicating Perfectionism

- A diamond with flaws is more precious than a perfect pebble. You are the diamond.
- To demand perfection is arrogance. It is like saying that there are losers out there that can be imperfect, but not me (Penzel, 202).

Living in the Moment

- Don't dig your own grave and attend your own

funeral while you are still alive.

- The past moments are ancient history and cannot be changed, and the future is uncertain, so live in the present moment. It is all you really have.
- Life is a terminal illness. Make the most of each day you are given.

Risk

- The biggest disasters take place in our imagination.
- Think of yourself as a scientist conducting experiments to see whether your disaster theories are correct (Penzel, 62).
- Life is inherently risky (Penzel, 62).
- The more you try to eliminate risk from your life, the less you will be able to function (Penzel, 32).
- If others don't see things as being risky in the way that you do, it is not because they are ignorant. You are off track, not the rest of the world (Penzel, 205).

Self-Acceptance

- Recognize your true identity; you are a child of God.
- OCD is just 3 letters. It does not define YOU.
- You are a unique being created by God, who loves you.

Self-Empowerment

- He who conquers himself is a better warrior than he who conquers a thousand men.
- You can be the 3 Cs – cool, calm, and collected.
- The same mind that can make you sick can make you well.
- You have choices in how you think.
- You don't have to be a slave to OCD thoughts.

Spirituality

- God is your ultimate healer.
- Greater is He that is within you, than the earthly world.
- Fear comes from you. Courage comes from the Divine that is within you.
- The fruit is already in the seed. (God's healing power is already within you; you just have to nurture it to make it grow.)
- God is Love (1 John 4:8).
- He who seeks his life will lose it; and he who loses his life for my sake will find it (*Matthew 10:39*).
- With man this is impossible, but not with God; all things are possible with God (*Mark 10:26-28*).

Tackling Fears

- Unless you have evidence, assume it is safe.

- Do what you fear.
- A man who fears suffering is already suffering from what he fears (French essayist Montaigne).
- When everything is contaminated, nothing is contaminated (Penzel, 63).
- Germs are everywhere.

Thought Life

- It is your attitude, not your aptitude that determines your altitude.
- The definition of a successful person is how high they bounce back after they are down.
- The only thing we have power over in the universe is our own thoughts (French philosopher Descartes).
- You cannot change what happens to you, but you can change your reaction to it.
- Spiritual thought, word and action is a lifelong process requiring practice. And the more you practice it, the better you get at it.

Works Cited

Bainton, Roland H. *Here I Stand: A Life of Martin Luther.* New York, Meridian, 1995.

Bassett, Lucinda. *From Panic to Power.* New York, HarperCollins, 1995.

Bell, Jeff. *Rewind, Replay, Repeat, A Memoir of Obsessive–compulsive Disorder.* Center City, MN, Hazelden, 2007.

"Brain Imaging Technologies." *Brain Imaging Technologies* University of Utah Genetic Science Learning Center, 30 June 2015, learn.genetics.utah.edu/content/neuroscience/brainimaging

Brand, Paul W., and Philip Yancey. *Fearfully and Wonderfully Made.* Grand Rapids, MI, Zondervan, 1980.

Cliff, Albert E. *Let Go and Let God: Steps in Victorious Living.* New York, Fireside Book, 1979.

Futrelle, David. "Can Money Buy Happiness?" *Money*, 18 July 2006, doi:10.1002/9781444305159.ch6.

Gallawa, Carlton J. "Safety of Microwave Energy – An Objective Discussion, This Site is Under Construction and Coming Soon." *Web Page Under Construction*, The Complete Microwave Oven Service Handbook: Operation, Maintenance, Troubleshooting and Repair, www.gallawa.com/microtech/Ch3.html. Accessed 1 Aug. 2017.

Grayson, Jonathan. *Freedom from Obsessive- compulsive Disorder: A Personalized Program for Living with Uncertainty.* New York,

Berkley Books, 2003.

Hallowell, Edward H. *Dare to Forgive: The Power of Letting Go and Moving on*. Deerfield Beach, FL, Health Communications, 2004.

Hankins, Scott, et al. "The Ticket to Easy Street? The Financial Consequences of Winning the Lottery." *By Scott Hankins, Mark Hoekstra, Paige Marta Skiba:: SSRN*, Vanderbilt Law and Economics Research Paper No. 10-12, 09 Jan. 2009, papers.ssrn.com/sol3/papers.cfm?abstract_id=1324845. Accessed 1 Aug. 2017

Ilardi, Stephen S. The Depression Cure: The 6-step Program to Beat Depression without Drugs. Cambridge, MA, Da Capo Lifelong, 2010.

Kinkade, Thomas. *Soul Care Bible/New King James version: Experiencing and Sharing Hope God's Way*. Thomas Nelson, 2001.

Levin, Jeffrey S. *God, Faith and Health: Exploring the Spirituality-healing Connection*. New York, Wiley, 2002.

Moskowitz, Clara. "Criminal Minds are Different from Yours, Brain Scans Reveal." *LiveScience*. Purch, 4. Mar. 2011, www.livescience.com/13083-criminals-brain-neuroscience-ethics.html. Accessed 1 Aug. 2017.

Nelson, Elizabeth A., et al. "Scrupulosity in Patients with Obsessive-Compulsive Disorder: Relationship to Clinical and Cognitive Phenomena." *Journal of Anxiety Disorders*, vol. 20, no. 8, 2006, pp. 1071–1086.,

Works Cited

doi:10.1016/j.janxdis.2006.02.001.

O'Callaghan, Tiffany. "A Neurological Explanation for the Placebo Effect?" *Time*, Time. 26 Aug. 2009, wellness.blogs.time.com/2009/08/26/a-neurological-explanation-for-the-placebo-effect/. Accessed 1 Aug. 2017

Osborn, Ian. *Can Christianity Cure Obsessive – compulsive Disorder? A Psychiatrist Explores the Role of Faith in Treatment.* Grand Rapids, MI, Brazos, 2008.

Osborn, Ian. *Tormenting Thoughts and Secret Rituals: The Hidden Epidemic of Obsessive-compulsive Disorder.* New York, Dell, 1999.

Penzel, Fred. *Obsessive–compulsive Disorders: A Complete Guide to Getting Well and Staying Well.* New York, NY, Oxford University Press, 2000.

Phillipson, Steven J. "God Forbid." *OCDonline.com,* 2016, www.ocdonline.com/god-forbid.

Phillipson, Steven J. "Speak of the Devil." *OCDonline.com*, 2016, www.ocdonline.com/speak-of-the-devil.

Phillipson, Steven J. "Thinking the Unthinkable." *OCDonline.com*, 2016, www.ocdonline.com/thinking-the-unthinkable.

Rapoport, Judith L. *The Boy Who Couldn't Stop Washing: The Experience and Treatment of Obsessive-Compulsive Disorder.* New York, Signet, 1991.

Robinson, B.A. "The Golden Rule (A.k.a. Ethics of Reciprocity)." *Versions of the Golden Rule in Dozens of Religions and Other Sources*, Ontario Consultants on Religious Tolerance, 1995, www.religioustolerance.org/reciproc2.htm.

Schwartz, Jeffrey M.D. *Brain Lock: Free Yourself from Obsessive-compulsive Behavior.* New York, HarperCollins, 1996.

Sears, Barry MD. *The Anti-Inflammation Zone: Reversing the Silent Epidemic That's Destroying Our Health.* New York, HarperCollins, 2005.

Seppala, Emma. "The #1 Shortcut to Greater Productivity." *Psychology Today*, Sussex Publishers, 7 Sept. 2016, www.psychologytoday.com/blog/feeling-it/201609/the-1-shortcut-greater-productivity.

Servan-Schreiber, David. *Anti-Cancer: A New Way of Life.* New York, Viking, 2009.

Stanley, Charles F. *A Gift of Love: Reflections for a Tender Heart.* Nashville, T. Nelson, 2001.

Stanley, Charles F. *Finding Peace: God's Promise of a Life Free from Regret, Anxiety and Fear.* Nashville, T. Nelson, 2003.

Stanley, Charles F. *How to Handle Adversity.* Nashville, T. Nelson, 1989.

Stanley, Charles F. *Put the Past behind You and give…The Gift of Forgiveness.* Nashville, T. Nelson, 1991.

Wade, Nicholas. "The Evolution of the God Gene." *The New York Times.* The New York Times, 14 Nov. 2009, www.nytimes.com/2009/11/15/weekinreview/12wade.html?_r=1&scp=1&sq=god+gene&st=nyt. Accessed 1 Aug. 2017.

"Winning the Lottery Isn't a Ticket to Happiness." CanWest Media Works Publications Inc., 5 May 2008.

Works Cited

www.canada.com/vancouversun/news/story.html?id=437ad1ca-df68-4472-91ad-2c57c7da8d6f&k=96500.

Worcester, WL, and H. Blackmer. "The Bible's Inner Meaning, Story by Story." *The Swedenborg Digital Library: Online Books about the Second Coming (Second Advent) of Jesus Christ, Revealed through Emanuel Swedenborg*. Swedenborg Project, 2012. www.swedenborgdigitallibrary.org/sower/mm/mk14.htm. Accessed 1 Aug. 2017.

www.ingramcontent.com/pod-product-compliance
Lightning Source LLC
Chambersburg PA
CBHW061318040426
42444CB00011B/2702